Sit Up and Stop Clowning Around

He Refused To Grow Up and
Recommends You Do The Same

By

Ronnie Carrington

Warning

This book has footnotes to explain things in a more clear, brief and succinct way. Ultimately, I had to add more words to make it more concise. I was told not to say the same thing over and over. To get to the point. Refrain from repeating myself. Leave only what is necessary on the page. Delete everything else. And that's what I'm going to do after this paragraph.

It is also a way for me to keep the book sanitized, sterile, and disinfected for those who may be offended by naughty words, vulgarity or cussing. You don't have to read the footnotes to understand the rest of the text. In fact, for some[1], it would be better not to read the footnotes, especially if the words and phrases like "shucks, bloomin, poo poo, dagnabbit, friggin or oh my gosh" upsets you in any way.[2] It's only going to get worse.

Finally, the footnotes gave me the chance to say what I really wanted to say in the first place. Consider the footnotes to be what I was thinking, but I never said. Hey, everybody thinks of stuff they know they should never say. Just remember, it's only a footnote.

---

[1] Some older people (90 plus), extremists, some religious people, the Pope (although not all of them), children three or under, the queen of England, and my mother. I am hoping my mother can take a little ribbing. She does have a good sense of humor. But she also does not approve of naughty words. I am either going to get a smile or a frown.

[2] You really should get that fixed. Go hang out with some sailors, pro athletes, comedians, politicians who think the mic is turned off, rock bands, most teenagers, non-religious people, most Hollywood folk, college students, or my wife.

Important Definitions

Clown (according to Merriam-Webster Dictionary):

a: a fool, jester, or comedian in an entertainment (such as a play) *specifically:* a grotesquely dressed comedy performer in a circus

b: a person who habitually jokes and plays the buffoon

My observation: How dare these Merriam-Webster people call what I wear grotesque?

How I would use it in a sentence: The biggest clown at the office is my boss.

Clown (according to many people I've met): Anybody who pisses them off when driving.

Used in a sentence: Can you believe that clown just cut me off?

Clown (according to me): Every human being who has and will ever live. Some are just more so.

Used in a sentence: Hey you reading this. Yes you. You're a damn clown too!!!!

Be proud of it.

Preface

A few years ago, I turned on my computer to access the book I had been writing since 2012. To my horror, the computer would not boot up. Instead, it flickered and then seemingly took its last breath before dying. I immediately took it to the computer hospital where, after attempting CPR, they confirmed it was indeed dead. I asked how that could happen and they told me the computer had crashed.

But I wasn't giving up. So, I asked the computer experts to remove the hard drive and place it in a new computer only to hear that everything that was on the hard drive was inaccessible and that I should just use my backup. Problem was, there was no back up. It was a hard drive home.

Have you ever worked on something for 10 years only to have all your work disappear? I felt like it was I who was about to crash. At minimum, my operating system was no longer functional, and my hard drive was corrupted. I was waiting for the blue screen of death.

The next few months were a mixture of anger, depression and despair. At times I would attempt my own version of computer CPR by blowing on the dust filled motherboard and compressing the computer's chest files. Eventually I resolved myself to being a wanna be writer without a book. When friends who knew I was writing would ask me how it was going I would respond, "It's going great," and then binge watch *Breaking Bad* to escape the torment.

A few years later when everyone had stopped asking me when my book was coming out, I built up enough gumption to get off the couch, turn off the TV and start writing again. The new book would be called *Why I Hate Computers.*

This time I knew to save my writing to an external hard drive, my laptop, USB, the cloud, the sky, the moon and the stars.

But the book I had written ten years earlier was still a part of me and I was not free to walk away. One day I told my wife the truth about why I was no longer working on the book, and she made a suggestion. That is, after making a scene. She asked me if I had ever sent a copy of the book via email to anyone. At first, I did not remember doing this. But as I thought about it, I realized that when I was about ¾ way through, I had sent a copy to a friend to help with editing. So, I nervously searched my email and found a copy of the book. It was a previous, less complete version. But it was a version. I was back in business. I had something to work with. I felt like I had been given a second chance and that it was time to finish the damn thing. I was so excited about this rough version of my writing that I sent it off to be printed so I could see what it might look like in book format. Then I ordered 5 copies of this almost finished, grammatically challenged, really rough version of my book. I figured I could give a copy to a few select people who I could trust to overlook the several errors I knew existed on almost every page. And have them promise never to show anyone else. Especially my mother. But life is funny sometimes. And very unpredictable. And my mother is very good at getting people to share their secrets.

P.S. If you have one of these copies please burn immediately.

Table Of Contents

Introduction

Which kid hasn't been told to sit up and stop clowning around? I certainly was. On a daily basis. By my parents, schoolteachers, uncles, aunts, older siblings, my boss, police officers, college professors and my wife. To start with, I was always a slouch. My father was constantly telling me to sit up. And clowning around was in my nature, silliness in my DNA. I was born to clown around. And I did.

Come with me on my journey from fun loving kid, wayward teenager, Bible college student, ordained minister, children's pastor, kids' magician, bunny enthusiast, videographer, part time clown and full-time kid. (I didn't list youth pastor because I am desperately trying to recover from that experience and cannot talk about it yet.)

Through the years, I came to see the thread that held everything together for me – funny stuff. Clowning around became my outlet, the way I dealt with boredom. In my world, laughter was the antidote to feeling bored and making someone giggle brought excitement.

From getting spanked for giving jokes in class, to having my father constantly correct my poor posture while I mimicked his face, I learned that we live in a very serious world with serious rules and serious consequences. My calling was to make it less so.

Over the years I came to accept that I was indeed different—a misfit of sorts. That my clowning around at times came at an expense, and that some wouldn't find me so damn funny. Clowning around, it turns out, is often fraught with danger. What I didn't realize was how difficult it would be to find my niche. And how important it was to believe in something.

But when I was at my lowest, two people came to my rescue. My father, who was no longer on this earth. And my wife, who is out of this world. It seemed they teamed up to help this silly guy realize how much he had to offer. That the evolution taking place in his life was not a revolution. There were talents not utilized. Potential, unfulfilled. A message not yet discovered. A book not yet written.

The line between silly and profound is blurred, but real. The ridicule for trying to be clever can be brutal. To be true to myself, I have to walk that thin line in hope that some will appreciate my essence, even as others question my intellect.

But one thing is certain. No matter how serious life gets, I'm not going to stop 'clowning around.'

Funny Confession

All the world's a stage,
And all men and women merely players;
They have their exits and their entrances;
And one man in his time plays many parts,
His acts being seven stages.
William Shakespeare's As You Like It

<u>Here is my take on this</u>

All the world's a stage
And all men and women will act
From birth till death
Each will embrace many roles
In seven stages
Ronnie Carrington's Like It or Not

I have a confession to make. I know I don't know you well enough to share my problems, and I understand it's risky to make myself vulnerable to strangers, but I gotta tell somebody my story or I may start talking to myself. Again.

Over the years, my compulsion to kid around has grown from being silly in kindergarten to being silly in church. Just for the record, I am not a circus clown. Couldn't find a college with a major in clowning around though several of them were clearly a circus.

I am a clown in the sense that I make people laugh. Sometimes, even intentionally. I perform comedy magic and ventriloquist acts at special events (mostly for kids) in front of a live audience in exchange for money. And free food at the buffet.

When I first started to perform professionally, I used to wear clown makeup, baggy polka-dotted pants, oversized converse clown shoes, and a red clown nose. Until I got tired of scaring many of my clients. Especially, the adults. Now I wear a beanie hat[3], regular-sized converse sneakers and rainbow suspenders.

When I was a kid, I would wait till my brother's face was filled with food to flick rice grains at mom, then watch as he laughed when I hit dad instead, the food spurting out his mouth. Dad didn't think it was so damn funny – which made it even funnier. That was when I discovered that playing with your food, while great entertainment for kids, was considered a serious crime to adults. Sit up and stop playing with your meatballs was the equivalent of – "Place your knife and fork on the table and hold your hands high above your head where we can see them." Then my parents would threaten to donate my food to the dogs, to which I would respond, "Is that a threat or a promise?"

Parents get very touchy when it comes to using food for anything other than the intended purpose. Something about wasting stuff rubbed them the wrong way. I didn't always share their sentiment. Especially when the food wasn't fit for human consumption, and I, being a human, would refuse to consume it. But knowing that all this fooling around at the table was absolutely forbidden added significantly to the level of entertainment. Plus, I knew that once my parents laughed at my antics, it would be almost impossible for them to discipline me.

Dinner time at the Carrington residence was a ritual that provided

---

[3] Colorful hat with a propeller on top that signifies one's playful attitude, silly disposition, and willingness to inflict great numbers with the giggles or suggests an adult who needs a serious mental evaluation.

me with a decent set of props (the food, drink, knife, fork, glass, and plate) and, most importantly, a captive audience – Mom, Dad, my younger brother, Tommy, and my older siblings, Richard and Rosie. During dinner, I would be corrected more in thirty minutes than I had the entire day. "Stop playing with your food, get your elbows off the table, you have your fork in the wrong hand, don't play with your knife; you're gonna poke somebody's eye out, don't talk with your mouth full, don't touch your brother, sit up and stop clowning around," were common directives given to me at supper. I never understood why my elbows touching the table was some type of serious crime worthy of stern punishment. Were my elbows toxic? The level of annoyance this act produced was disproportionate to any actual infraction. At least "don't play with your knife" came with a reasonable explanation, i.e., some human being may lose an eye.

The day I found out that it was possible to burp on command, I thought I discovered the holy grail of supper antics. I knew this newfound talent would stimulate much snickering at the table and provide me with something I could someday pass down to my nephews and nieces. Which I'm happy to report I did. You're welcome.

Both Mom and Dad took their parenting job very seriously and tried hard to break me of my societal indiscretions, and I did a very good job of resisting them.

I was always one of those kids who asked a heck of a lot of questions and often felt like I wasn't getting decent answers. For some reason, I just didn't take what people said as fact. Call me skeptical, but when things didn't make sense to me, I had the audacity to say so.

"Why not?" and "Who says?" were two of my favorite questions, and "Because I say so" was my least favorite answer. Like when my mom said, "Don't place your elbows on the dinner table," I would ask, "Why not?"

Then she would say something about it not being proper etiquette, and I would ask, "Who says?"

"Don't tease your baby brother."

"Why not?"

"Don't stick that coat hanger in the electrical socket." (The answer to this one was quite shocking.)

"Don't sit so close to the TV." "Why not?"

"Because you'll go blind."

Who says?" (They didn't have Google back in those days or I would have shown my mom that this was actually not factual.)

"Don't curse."

"Why the hell not?"

Some people saw my questioning as being a bad thing. Others thought I just needed a good whoopin'. It could have been that I was just a curious kid filled with wonder. But more than likely, I just needed the good whoopin'. Fortunately, both my parents were there to fulfill those needs.

But I never did stop clowning around. At school, I was known to gather a small group of fifth graders and boldly recite – milk, milk, lemonade, round the corner fudge is made, while pointing to the teacher's two knockers (milk), down below (lemonade) and then butt (fudge). Almost all my comedy routines as a kid contained material not suitable for adults. They would have washed out my mouth with soap.

In the years I was growing up, parents and schoolteachers still believed in corporal punishment, and I was "corporaled" many times. You could say many of my educators have tried to beat the silly out of me. Fortunately, they failed, and I still have lots of silly left. But I wasn't looking for trouble. I just wanted to be funny and was willing to risk punishment to do so. Seeing a huge smile on the face of my ten-year-old school friends, and knowing it was I who created this visual was deeply gratifying. Unfortunately, none of my teachers found my clowning around amusing, and this added significant risk to my routines. The pressure was great preparation for what I do now for a living – professional live comedy since my teachers could cause me pain, not dissimilar to the pain caused by a heckler. Both are a pain in the ass.

My father was one of the most unclowny people I knew. Everything about him was serious. From the way he sat up straight, to his perfectly spoken English, he was not one to fool around. He was one of the few people I knew who, when described as standing 6 foot tall, really did justice to the word tall. Even if he was 3 feet, it most certainly would have been tall. When he stood up, his body was perfectly straight, his shoulders perpendicular to the ground as if calculated with a compass. His chest, extended outward and reaching for the sky, was set on top of a perfectly thin waistline. My posture, by contrast, sucked.

His head was the perfect visual for what was meant by "hold your head high," and when he put on his dark glasses, the resulting figure was striking in the way male lions standing on an African plain are magnificent. His face was movie-star handsome, with a sharp Clark Gable-like jawbone and blue eyes that were somewhat unusual for someone with his dark olive-like complexion. It was as if God had made a human based on a recipe that called for a blend of several races, tribes, and nationalities, and the mixture produced an exotic, striking visual that could be universally appreciated. Having said that, I know I am completely biased since I too, have a similar, if not equally impressive physicality. But in my case, I have managed to mask any attractiveness by simply adding an extra bowling ball (or three) in weight and by neglecting to groom even one square inch of my body. Add that I tend to wear the type of clothing that house painters use to stop the paint from staining their skin, and you have a man who is not usually mistaken for handsome, except by maybe his wife, who tends to see the potential in people.

I remember looking up at my father and feeling so small and weak in comparison. My earliest memories of conversation included several directives to improve my apparently poor posture. I believe I can even remember hearing my dad instruct me to sit up when I was in my mother's womb. As important as it was to him to stand tall, it was almost impossible for me to even sit without slouching. I wasn't trying to be non-compliant; it just wouldn't register in my brain that there was anything wrong with the way I was sitting.

"How many times do I have to tell you to sit up straight?" He would snap at me while I was busy placing a pea at the end of my fork and preparing to sling it across the table at my younger brother, Tommy. In my head, I would pick a random number and whisper it under my breath, "678?" If he heard me, of course, I would be in trouble.

I cannot tell you how many times my dad tried to get me to stop walking with my feet turned out. He thought that was completely unacceptable. He wanted me to walk with my shoulders straight, my head up, and my feet pointed in the direction I was walking. I, by some curse of the gods, would walk much more like Charlie Chaplin, except I wasn't trying to be funny. In the end, no matter how much my father wanted to raise a distinguished gentleman, what he got was a clumsy clown. Almost everything about my posture shouted "sloppy," and I finally came to accept myself as hopeless. First of all, my hair was always too long and had just enough curls so that it grew in all different directions with varying lengths. If it wasn't glued down with mousse or hair spray, neither of which I used, it looked like a bird's nest, which is exactly what my 7th grade class called me while adding that birds were going to lay eggs in my head. My shirt seemed unwilling to stay in my pants, as if the tucked-in ends could not breathe and had to jump out for air, and the shirt was often buttoned out of sequence so that one end was longer than the other. Taking the time to put on a belt was clearly not a priority to me, and it was a good thing my trousers fell down on my hip so that the pant bottoms could hide the fact that I had elected not to wear socks. Getting me to shine my shoes would be the equivalent of getting a mule to gallop across the desert, and it wasn't unusual for my feet to be covered with two different types of sneakers. (Who had time to check?) I did at least wear clean underwear whenever I had any, and I have always remembered the advice given me by a similarly slob-leaning school friend that I could always turn my briefs inside out if I wanted to re-wear them. Even when I was dressed up for some special event like a wedding, it wouldn't be long before I looked like I had just done a live news broadcast on a hurricane in progress while standing in the storm.

Dad and I had completely opposite views of what was important. It is not surprising that we had a strained relationship at times. Our contrasting posture was symbolic of our opposing worldviews, and I rebelled against his insistence that I take life seriously and felt that he should take it less so.

I would often wonder how parents arrived at the list of vital rules their children would be forced to follow and why posture was so important. Would slouching kill me someday? And which party pooper came up with no running in the house? So you might lose a few heirloom vases to a speeding toddler, or the Bone China set to a nine-year-old missing a turn. Wasn't it more important for us children to have fun? And there was no doubt in my mind that making us kids kiss the relatives we visited was a rule that constituted cruel and unusual punishment. And before you trivialize my opinion on this, consider a six-year-old boy who was forced to hug and kiss his 80-year-old grand aunt who had large bumps all over her face and arms. I am sure she was a lovely lady but couldn't I just wave at her from the car?

Trust me when I tell you that failing to kiss any of the adults we were visiting was a crime punishable by up to 15 minutes of berating plus making us go back and kiss the previously unkissed, bumpy grand aunt. And for some mysterious reason, no one was ever able to get it through my thick skull to say please and thank you every time somebody did something for me. It seemed that adults had some sort of unspoken code that compelled them to inform each other if any of their children failed to say the magic words.

Every Saturday, my brother and I went to see a double feature movie at a local movie theater owned by a family relative. The tickets for us were free. And every Saturday, we went home to hear my mother ask, "Why didn't you tell Mrs. Picky thank you for the tickets she handed you?" Apparently, Mrs. Picky had called my mom to inform her I didn't say thank you. I so wanted to say, "Because I don't think that handing me movie tickets deserves a thank you. It's Mrs. Picky's job to hand out movie tickets. She doesn't own the movie theater." Of course, that was the wrong answer. "Sorry Mom, it won't ever happen again," was the right answer, no matter how disingenuous it might have been. My mom was determined to teach me to act as if I was thankful, even when I was clearly not.

The rules when I was growing up seemed endless, without logic, and certainly not child friendly. Take for instance, "Don't touch that." When I was two years old, touching things was my whole life. I lived to touch things. I mean, how many conversations would I have been able to handle at two, and how many activities does a toddler have on their calendar? When I opened my eyes in the morning, my preschool brain was thinking, "What can I touch today? Oh look, Dad's prescription medicine. Maybe I'll see what it tastes like."

But the dinner table was my favorite place to touch things and push the limits of what I could get away with. A place where living right at the edge of what was forbidden and what was funny gave me creative license and made me feel alive. Clowning around was a balancing act in which my careful breaking of the rules would be tolerated, even appreciated, especially if it provoked a laugh or even a smile from the adults in charge of my nurturing. It was a place where one unfunny action could be met with frowns or maybe even punishment. But I was up for the challenge. I had no idea at the time the type of world I was going to face and the complicated path my love for humor would take me on. All I knew was I really had a hard time sitting up.

And under no circumstances was I going to retire clowning around.

My Big Entrance

At first the infant,
Mewling and puking in the nurse's arms;
William Shakespeare's As You Like It

<u>Here is my take on this</u>

At first, your mom will hand you to the nurse
Because you are bringing up shit!
Ronnie Carrington's She Don't Like It

My clown journey started February 9, 1959, the day I was born Christopher John Carrington. Right after officially choosing my beautiful, well-thought-out name and formally documenting it on my birth certificate, my parents immediately began calling me Ronnie for reasons I will discuss in my next book called, *What the Hell Were They Thinking?* The important thing to note is that this strange choice has led to more than 25% of my life spent trying to explain why the name on my driver's license did not match the name everybody in the world calls me and 10% of my life tracking down people who gave me checks made out to the non-existent Ronnie Carrington. It has also led to some very interesting banter with police officers looking at my driver's license while hearing my brother repeatedly refer to me as Ronnie. It is of some consolation to me that my parents did the same thing to my younger brother, Patrick, who everyone knows as Tommy. This eliminates the excuse that my parents just had a really off day.

My birth took place in a hospital located in Kingston, Jamaica. I am pretty sure of my parent's race because I recently spent hundreds of dollars checking our family tree on the internet. They are part of what's known as – 'the human race,' although I do acknowledge it is entirely possible they were mixed with something else. To be more specific, I can tell you that we all have one belly button and skin all over our bodies. You could ask my brothers for a description of what is underneath my skin – they spent a lot of time getting under it.

My mom told me that elders from their church suggested we had a nice home with lots of rooms, but it needed a small human being and my dad was up for the challenge. When I think about why I was born, sometimes I am convinced it was God who predestined me to be here before the foundations of the earth. At other times, I think it was just pure chance. Then, I reason that I was just the fastest sperm in my particular group. Most likely, however, it is a combination of all of the above, depending on who I am talking to.

Sitting in my Mom's stomach was similar to sitting in a warm jacuzzi having unlimited nourishment and absolute privacy. I'm so glad my mom didn't have twins. I'm not very good at sharing small spaces with other people.

During this time in my life, I was very close to my mom's heart and even closer to her fallopian tubes, ovaries, and uterus. I remember I was somewhat nervous about entering the world's stage and wondering how I would be received. Lots of things can go wrong on any journey into the limelight, especially one with such a narrow hallway and critical audience.

The day I was to make my grand entrance, my mother was rushed to the hospital and her entourage followed. I am told that my arrival was highly anticipated. She was whisked into a room and her feet were placed in the double swing set. Then the curtains opened, and my mom pushed me out into the spotlight and onto the world stage…along with a potpourri of liquids, gasses, and soft solids. It was a miracle of sorts, a sight to behold, a spectacular opening act. One moment, the room had three humans, and then, like magic, abracadabra, there were four. Tadaaaa! As soon as I arrived on stage, I got smacked on the ass by some clown wearing a mask over his mouth and nose. Maybe he didn't want to be recognized. It hurt like hell, so I cried, and the audience seemed pleased with my performance. Everybody clapped, giving me my first standing ovation and I could tell I was the star of the show, and this was some show. For starters, I was totally naked, which must have been a real treat for the ladies.

In those early minutes, I had a really solid connection with the main lady in my life – my mother. Then, suddenly, the doctor with the mask cut the cord, and it was the beginning of my solo act. I was only a few minutes old but was already alone in the cold world of competition without any connections, and this inspired more crying.

They wrapped me in my first costume, not much more than a piece of cloth, and then handed me to the lady who had just pushed me out from her dressing room. I can imagine the look on my mom's face as she checked me out for imperfections. I have now seen that look for more than 60 years. Her laser-like stare, with furrowed eyebrows and puckered mouth, betraying her critical thoughts. She made me feel subpar, even disappointing. Oh, I'm sure I looked normal enough. Two eyes, two ears, two arms, one nose, one asshole, and most important … one penis. A body part that seemingly needed reshaping. Because that's what they did. Trimmed it back. As if I didn't need all of it.

I am pretty sure my mom found something wrong with me, compared me to my older brother and sister and then told everybody how I was flawed.

My hair was probably too curly, or my ears too big. Maybe my head was too small – not enough brains. Other negative comments about my nose, lips, complexion, personality, abilities, poor eating habits, and lack of proper etiquette were probably discussed. My mom offered my first professional critique. She rarely liked anyone's performances besides her own. "Nurse, you can take him to the nursery room now. He's starting to drool," I imagine her saying. "What a mess he's making." Then, off I went to a room with a bunch of other little clowns. Most of them were crying and none of them looked happy to be in the show of their life. I am sure they stared at me with an expression that expressed contempt. I was, after all, taking some of their breathing air.

It seemed like the show was going to be a real challenge, a mixture of pain and pleasure, joy and sadness, good and bad acts with a really difficult ending. This living-in-the-world thing was to be a real circus. In these early stages, I had a lot of questions. Where's my mommy? What kind of place is this? What's up with all these strange people? What is my purpose for being here? What should I do for a living? Why does my penis hurt so much, and where is the rest of it?[4]

Then, they brought out the makeup crew, and cleaned me up so I would look more presentable for the other people who were arriving to see my act. In those early hours of my show, it was crying, sleeping, or making milk in a bottle disappear, but the audience didn't seem to care what I did. It was all good.

Later, they took me to a man who shared many of my features, and he looked pleased. All I needed to do for this dude was to breathe, and he was all smiles. He tried to get me to call him daddy, but I wanted him to prove himself first. At least be around for a few years. You know, take care of all my needs.

---

[4] They just threw it away.

A few days later, when my parents took me home, I discovered that there were already two other clowns living at my house. My older brother Richard was eight and always on center stage. His acting up was legendary, and my mother has told me stories of the many times he was chased around by my dad with a belt. It wasn't to hold up his pants. Apparently, Richard would threaten to break "somekin" and my parents didn't want "anykin" broken. Richard's act consisted of anything he could think of to get attention, and he was good at it. The attention he would get, however, often produced frowns, groans, and pleas for him to stop it, but unfortunately, this did not seem to deter him. The frequent running from my parents may have contributed to Richard eventually setting several high school running records. He could run at a pace just fast and long enough to where your average adult would eventually give up the chase.[5]

My sister, Rosie, was also a great performer and often attempted to upstage my brother by being way too adorable. At her third birthday party, she was dressed in a frilly skirt with frilly panties and frilly bows, and my brother wanted to soak her with the hose. I am sure he thought that no one should be allowed to be that 'frilly.' The look on his face from the birthday pictures in our family album shows him glaring at her. My parents knew they had two very good-looking children and proceeded to decorate them like you would a Christmas tree.

"How adorable. Cute as a button. What beautiful children. So handsome. Look at the frills."

Rosie and Richard had more than six years of being on center stage before I arrived and started messing up their act. They thought they had a two-person show with an air-tight, no-other-clown

---

[5] 440 yards, Richard's first distance running record.

contract. Knowing what I know now about them, I am pretty sure they were apprehensive of my intentions. After all, Mom and Dad were now giving me a lot of attention.

A few times each day, I got everybody to respond immediately by pushing really hard and filling my diaper with that chocolate mush that came out of my tush. Boy, did that feel good. You should have seen the look on everyone's face. I knew it was a real crowd-pleaser by the speed with which they did a wardrobe change. Makeup. Then somebody would clean and powder my ass.

Very early on, I noticed that if I wanted everybody's undivided attention, all I had to do was open my mouth and make the most piercing sound I could produce with my brand-new vocal cords. It helped to add tears to the tantrum. It would not only bring the whole cast running to figure out what I wanted, but it would also get me picked up and held, along with a much-appreciated back patting massage. Having figured this out, I used this showstopper when Mom was paying too much attention to the other two clowns in our act.

Sometime later, my parents put me in a silly carriage with huge wheels and a convertible top, and this allowed me to take my show on the road. Being the star of the show, I could do no wrong. I never got spanked or scolded for anything. I could spit up, poop, piss and cry without consequence. Even when I drooled all over my daddy, he just wiped off his suit and spoke to me in a silly voice. "How is my little baby Ronnie doing? You wanna come to Da Da?" Sometimes, I just smiled, showing off my perfect set of gums, and puked all over his white shirt again. What else could I do with total impunity? Then, I realized that liquids could squirt out of my little hose down below, and with this secret weapon, I had some level of accuracy. If my older brother came too close to my crib, I knew exactly how to piss him off.

As the star of the show, it was in my contract that my needs would be taken care of. All room and board were included. My mom and the nanny continued to feed me with milk that came out of a bottle, although I did hear rumors that there was a much more fun way to be fed. In fact, it was said that when my older brother Richard was a baby, he had been fed directly from the two big round balloons that were attached to my mom's chest. My sources tell me that this feeding method was canceled for some undisclosed reason. I have my people working on the facts even as I write this account. [6]

During this early stage of my career, I was always the life of the party, the main attraction. People came to our home just to see me, and I didn't have to do much to get laughter and applause. Sometimes, I would wiggle my body and shake to the music that was playing.

My dad, always the ultimate ringmaster, made sure everybody in our circus was acting appropriately, occasionally cracking his whip if anybody got out of line. Sometimes, when my nine-year-old brother was being a real animal, my dad had to crack his ass with his whip to get him to comply. Then, Dad made my brother jump through hoops like doing his homework, lying down, and going to sleep at bedtime.

I was about a year old when my dad started working with me on my acrobatic act. He would throw me in the air and catch me over and over. I was terrified he would drop me, and it would be the end of my career, but no one was asking for my opinion of these dangerous stunts. Sometimes, he swung me around in a circle until I felt like bringing up my Gerber green pea lunch. I must admit it was sometimes fun being thrown in the air and spun around like that, and I often giggled, which only seemed to encourage the man to do

---

[6] My mom confirmed my brother was breastfed for a while but won't disclose the reason for the cancellation of this feeding program.

more training.

On one occasion, I remember someone placed me directly on an ant nest so that they could take a photo of my little chubby body. I am assuming it was by accident, but the expression I had in that image should have been a dead giveaway that something was wrong with this picture. Planted on my plump round face was an expression of deep concern and thoughtful agony, and my arms were outstretched in a cry for somebody to get me off of whatever was eating at me.

My acting skills during the first year of my life were impeccable. You could hardly tell I was acting at all. Everything I did seemed to come naturally. The laughs, the smiles, the frowns, and the wonder in my eyes were without pretense. It would take years to learn how to be fake.

My First Big Break

And then the whining school-boy, with his satchel
And shining morning face, creeping like snail
Unwillingly to school.
William Shakespeare's As You Like It

Here is my take on this

And then the whining kid
Going slow
Because he hates school
Ronnie Carrington's As You Don't Like It

My first day of preschool did not start out well. It was the first time I would have to spend my whole damn day with a bunch of little clowns. I was probably about 28 months old, maybe 29. Okay, 30 – tops.

The owner of the school was Miss Andrews, my Godmother. I had no idea what that meant at the time, but now that I am a grown, mature adult, I am even more confused. Was she God's mother, a godly mother, a mother god recommended, a god to mothers, a fairy godmother, a holy mother of God? Who the hell was she? Godfather, I get. He is the man who tells everybody else in an Italian family what to do. And if it was the Godfather from an Italian family, you had better damn well do what he says, or you might end up meeting God, your father.

I remember my mom driving up to school and having the sneaky suspicion that she was going to try and actually leave me there. She parked the car, walked me up to the entrance, and then attempted to hand me over to my new teacher. I was crying uncontrollably. The type of cry that causes a child to hyperventilate and act like they're dying. I am sure I added in a few coughs and snorts for effect. I wanted to make it clear that I was completely opposed to this transfer from my mom to the lady with the gruff voice. I don't know you, I thought. You could be dangerous. She was. Maybe you believe in spanking little children. She did. What if you try to make me do things I hate? She would.

"Mom, please, do not leave me with this lady. I don't think I'm gonna like her," I tried communicating with agonizing wails. Doesn't it take time to get to know people? I thought. I was just a little guy, but I was strong enough that my hands, firmly locked around my Mommy's neck, could not be budged except maybe by the Navy Seals and a large jaws of life type device. Plus, I thought this was a life and death situation, and at this point in my life, I still wanted to live. By now, my mom was running out of options, and all I could see was a mess of tangled blond hair and clenched lips. Some other overwhelmed mother might have given up and just taken their kid home. Other parents might have tried to pacify their child.

"Now there my little Poopsie, did the lady scare you? Don't worry, Mommy is not going to leave you if you don't want to stay," I can imagine some mother saying to her kid.

But that was not my mom. She doesn't do 'pacify.' My Mom looked right into my little blue eyes − and lied.[7]

"Ronnie, I am going to get the car and come back for you," she promised. "Just hang on to the lovely lady, and I will go get the car."

---

[7] This refers to the communication of information that is not entirely accurate for the protection, betterment, and advancement of small children who do not know better and cannot otherwise be motivated to comply with parental instruction. Please note that when sed parent insists that mothers never lie − they are full of shit.

I let go and went to the scary lady. Mom left and I did not see her again for eight hours.

I spent that day playing with my new friends and getting to know Miss Andrews. My new school room was filled with all types of little things. Little chairs, little tables, little cups, little portable toilet, little books, and little corners to sit in. They gave me snacks and played records with stories about a race between a very fast rabbit and a very slow turtle. Can you believe the turtle won? The rabbit took too many breaks. I think he had attention deficit disorder and possibly needed medication. Then, we used these really cool colored pencils to make some boring drawings come alive. All I had to do was try to stay within the lines, which was quite a feat for me. Then we had a nap time. This was great because I was really tired from all the crying, fighting with my mom, and dealing with all these new people. One kid kept bothering me, so I pushed him down to the ground, and apparently, this was not allowed in this joint. I had to sit on a chair in the little corner for five big minutes.

But the rules in this place were pretty loose. I was allowed to walk around and touch things, play with toys, communicate with other kids, and run around outside. I even got paint all over my hands, and the teacher was good with that.

When my mom finally came to pick me up, I didn't want to go home. This place was awesome. What I realized that day about my mom, I still appreciate. My mom is really an excellent liar, a true professional. Her performances are flawless. She can have a look on her face that completely betrays her real feelings. This is probably where I get much of my performance skills from. My dad, on the other hand, could not lie to save his life.

Not long after I started preschool, I performed my first acrobatic show. I was playing in the jungle gym outside with several of my three-year-old friends. One of them dared me to jump from a ledge to a bar about four feet away. It looked really dangerous, but when my friends started calling me chicken, I was filled with bravery.

"I dare you to do it," Mikey said. I looked at the distance and tried to judge my leaping ability. I was wrong. I recall thinking it was going to be close just before I jumped and missed the bar, falling at least eight feet to the ground and breaking my left arm. I probably remember this incident so well because of the excruciating pain and the subsequent trip to the hospital. My act drew a large crowd. You could say it was my first big break. When I was admitted to the hospital, I ended up sharing a room with my mother, who was also admitted at the same exact time, although I am not sure what she broke.

When I was forty-four months old, something very upsetting happened. My mom and dad brought home another clown. I thought it was in my contract that I worked alone, that I was always to be on center stage, the spotlight on me and me only. I had worked so diligently to get the other two clowns living with us relegated to supporting roles, and now I was going to have to compete with this clown. The day he walked onto my stage, I knew there was going to be trouble. Nobody was watching my act anymore, and everybody was gathered around 'Tommy.' Or 'Baby T' as my mom would affectionately call him. He was the new baby on the block. He was an 8 lb. 6 oz. bundle of joy or, as I would prefer to put it, "pain in the ass." The minute he arrived, he started stealing the show. First of all, just for the record, most of his act was taken from mine. He did the same 'trying to look cute' routine, the identical crying act, and can you believe he had the audacity to smile when my mom rocked him back and forth? I wanted to rock him, too. But I planned on using real rocks.

I was barely four years into my life, and it seemed as if my show was over. My baby brother had taken over my act. I knew he was gonna cause trouble, and he was only sixty-three hours old. But that look on his face. He looked like he needed to be slapped. I knew what he was up to. I was onto him. The low-down, dirty scumbag. Looking all cute and stuff. He was determined to get my parents to pay more attention to him than they did to me. And it worked. He was good.

Soon, Tommy would start to get on my nerves, and I would be forced to go into my taunting and teasing act complete with name calling. "Tommy is a baby, Tommy is a baby," I would chant. Then he would start crying, and I would get into trouble. Of course, he was a baby, but that's beside the point. He didn't have to advertise it so often. He used that 'I'm the cute-baby-brother-card' extremely effectively over the years, and my mom kept falling for it. Just a few months ago, my mom told me she had to console 'Baby T' by taking him on a short vacation because I had hurt his little feelings. At sixty-plus years old, he's still competing for my mother's affection and trying to discredit me. I envision both of us over eighty, my mom still alive at one hundred and eighteen years, and Tommy telling her, "Mom, Ronnie is teasing me again. He's calling me an old man."

"Ronnie, were you teasing Baby T? Don't call him an old man."

"But Mom, he is an old man," I would insist just before hiding his walker. "Hey, Tommy! Go put in your teeth before you complain to mom about anything else, you big baby."

After my brother took over my show, I became somewhat more introverted, even solemn. I had to retire my crying act completely. When I cried, nobody gave a s%*t. They had more important people to attend to – my baby brother. I remember that even my sister was now attending to my younger brother as though she was his personal manager. She was now twelve years old and apparently wanted one of these little bundles of joy for herself. Who could resist wanting to hold Tommy, cuddle Tommy, feed Tommy, and play with Tommy? Ronnie, on the other hand, could walk up and down the street, in traffic, at rush hour, on the highway, and nobody would notice. I know – I tried it.

On the other hand, if Tommy so much as sneezed, all personnel residing at 17 Dillsbury Avenue were to immediately report to Tommy's crib. I have seen several pictures of my sister holding her baby brother Tommy and looking at him with deep love and affection. No pictures of my sister looking at me. The bonding that took place between my sister and her brand-new baby brother was both touching and absolutely disgusting. I am told by very reliable sources that she had consulted with my parents about obtaining an additional sibling sometime earlier. She wanted a baby sister, but a baby boy was produced instead. So, she probably just pretended he was a baby sister. That would explain the floral, bright pink, and yellow clothes he was paraded in, although it would not explain why I was also paraded in the exact same floral clothes. What I know for a fact is that she was very protective of him and guarded him like he was her child.

Serious Trouble

Getting into trouble has always come naturally to me. The things I would think of doing seemed innocent enough, but trouble was often lying in wait. I contend that I did not deserve to suffer as I often did for my actions. Life was just cruel and unfair, and the rules were not always clear. Even if there were Ten Commandments given to us by God, these rules did not cover stuff I thought of doing. Thou shalt not try to catch a scorpion, thou shalt not play soccer in the living room, thou shalt not hide your brother's blanket, or thou shalt not throw rocks at abandoned cars were either overlooked or considered too obvious.

About six years into my life, there were signs that my healthy imagination and a willingness to do things that popped into my head without much consideration for consequences would lead to problems. While my little brother was quite happy to just walk the straight and narrow, I preferred to run it, occasionally making my own crooked path.

One day, my baby brother and I were in our backyard playing in our sandbox, and I noticed three old beat-up cars in an open lot behind our house. My playful imagination was stirred. Wouldn't it be fun to pick up some rocks and hurl them at the junk cars? I thought. I shared my plan with my little brother. He agreed to my bright idea. We gathered a bunch of the largest rocks that we could find and made a pile. Then I told my brother that the rocks were our weapons, the cars were invading monsters. The vehicles were nineteen fifty-something Chevys with big headlamps for eyes and a grill that was clearly making a mean face at us.

"We are Monsters from the Motorcar planet. We are going to take over Earth and eat you!" I imagined they said.

"Look, you Monster cars, my superhero baby brother and I will not allow you to take over the world! We will stop you. Return to your planet or prepare to be annihilated." The cars refused our order. We were forced to take further action. I gave the order to prepare for battle to my thirty-two-inch, twenty-eight-pound baby brother. It was in the days when I could give him an order, and he would obey. No questions asked.

"Load the cannons!" I shouted.

Tommy picked up a big rock and stood in the throw position. "Cannons loaded, Sir," he responded. I am sure he didn't say Sir, but it feels really good to write that he did.

"Ready. Aim. Fire!"

We both started hurling these rocks at the three invading Chevys in a merciless barrage. The monster cars didn't stand a chance. I don't think any of the rocks my brother threw actually hit anything. He was never good at throwing, catching, boxing, or anything in which coordination was required. Unfortunately, I was pretty darn accurate at this activity. Rocks were crashing through the windows, making huge dents in the doors, the hood, and the trunk.

"Psshhhh, vaboom, blooom, rat tat tat tat," we were both creating the sounds of battle with our mouths. Then I told my brother to pretend he was hit by enemy fire. It is entirely possible that at that point, I punched him in the chest so he could better simulate being wounded, but I am not admitting to that.

"Mayday, mayday, man down, man down, request air support." "Ssssssswwwwwwwwshhhhhhh." The air support flew overhead and dropped the killer bombs. We both threw our final volley of rocks.

The battle was over; the monster cars were defeated, the earth was saved, and we were in very big trouble.

How were we to know that those three Chevys were purchased by my father because he needed the spare parts for several cars he was restoring? The windshields alone were worth hundreds of dollars, not to mention the doors, the two lights that I had imagined were eyes steering us down, and the grill that now looked like a smiling mouth with several teeth knocked out.

When my dad came home and saw the remnants of our successful battle, he was not interested in why I felt the need to destroy the cars from outer space. Nor did he seem thankful that my brother and I had saved the planet. My sister watched from a distance as my dad sat my brother and me down for part one of our punishment. I don't remember seeing her during our trial and sentencing, but she knows a lot about what happened next, so I assume she was eavesdropping. My dad pronounced the charges against us.

Throwing rocks – guilty as charged.

Destruction of private property – guilty as charged.

Messing with the landscaped yard (there were now a lot of missing rocks) – guilty as charged.

Leading little brother to do bad things – guilty as charged.

Aiding and abetting (That was charged to my baby brother)

I can feel my sister wanting to say, "Objection, your honor, the accused was threatened into complying."

Then came the sentencing. Five lashes with the belt to the butt for Ronnie. Three lashes with the belt to the butt for Tommy. To my sister, the lashes handed down to Tommy were three lashes too many. In her mind, my dad should have added the three lashes meant for Tommy and applied them to Ronnie. I really don't hold that against her. He was only three years old. Plus, I have to confess this was really all my idea. He was just following my directions. Which, come to think of it, might explain why he no longer wants to follow me. In my opinion, the whole thing was just a big misunderstanding. I never meant to cause the destruction of valuable possessions. I thought the cars were junk. The rock throwing, I figured at the time, was completely harmless and would be lots of fun. But after the five lashes, my ass hurt so bad I knew that from that day forward, all battles against invading Monster cars would have to be fought by other battalions.

My brother and I were resigning our posts in the pretend military. This battle game became a royal pain in the ass.

After my throwing stage was over, I graduated to work with a wild and dangerous animal – our pet cat, Tabby. Okay, she was not that dangerous, but I assure you she was wild. She had very sharp claws and teeth that could kill and devour lizards and rats. I would see her with half a creature inside her mouth while the other half wiggled and squirmed, trying to escape from her powerful jaws. She didn't seem to care what the animal rights people thought about causing slow, agonizing death and would often play with her half-dead prey just for the heck of it. I became an expert at taming the terrifying Tabby. I would play with her each day after school, running with a piece of rope as she chased me all around our backyard. When she would catch the rope, I would pull it upwards into the air and watch in amazement at her ability to hang on, her sharp claws firmly embedded in the fiber. Tabby and I were inseparable mainly because those same claws were often embedded in my pants.

Then, one day, my mom called me aside to talk. I knew it was something that wasn't good because of her even-more-than-usual serious demeanor. "I'm sorry, Ron," Mom announced, "Tabby has passed away."

"Passed away? What do you mean? Where is she?" I didn't understand what Mom meant by either passed or away.

"She ate some rat poison and died," Mom explained.

I pondered this for a while. At six, death is perplexing. Not like adults who have it all figured out. My parents had not yet explained heaven to me. In any case, I now know that kitty heaven was nowhere to be found in the Bible. Thus, clearly does not exist. After a few minutes of silence, I saw that my mom looked sad and needed comforting.

"It's okay, Mom, don't feel bad. I'll keep Tabby on my toy shelf. I can hug her up at night."

It wouldn't be the last time I was confused about how life and death work. But over time, the big people would explain all of this to me.

Circus Memories

By the time I was in elementary school, I had established a pattern of fooling around in class, making fun of my teachers, giggling at the school principal's large mole on her right cheek, and throwing wads of paper at my fellow classmates. Sometimes, I used a rubber band to sling the small piece of paper at the back of a kid's neck. Then, when I hit the intended target, the kid would turn around, and I would pretend to be reading my textbook. That was great practice for future clown acts in which I would bop another clown on the head with a big plastic bat and then pretend it wasn't me. I did a lot of pretending in school as a child, including pretending to listen.

Personally, I found the lessons teachers were talking about as interesting as a snail race but with less excitement. While the teachers were pontificating, I would occupy myself by thinking of what I wanted to do after school. Things like playing marbles, going to a movie, playing with my pet cat, and teasing my baby brother. By teasing, I mean keeping him in line. He was always getting out of the lunch line at school to ask me for lunch money. My dad had given me the money to keep for him since I was the older, more responsible sibling. Being older and having more money than my brother should have meant he would do what I told him, but he was always stubborn. To this day, he still resists listening to me. But I am not giving up all hope.

One day, when I was in elementary school, I remember that I had not been able to recite my times table. Miss Brown, my teacher at the time, had given me a homework assignment to learn the times table. After school, I walked home, which was less than a block away and spent my entire afternoon playing with my best friend.

I went to school the next day without doing my homework. Miss Brown was a mean old teacher whose look would scare the crap out of you even when she was smiling. And she seldom smiled. She was born to scare children into doing their schoolwork. Sometimes when I knew I was in trouble, I would get the kind of sick feeling that gives you diarrhea, except it feels more like you have to fart. At times I wasn't sure if the fart was gas or soft liquid, and on occasion, I would make the fateful decision to push only to discover that it was indeed a soft liquid.

The next day at school, Miss Brown asked me to come up to the front of the class.

"Carrington," my teacher called out for all the kids to hear. "I hope you completed your homework assignment." I had not. She asked me to recite my times table. I could not.

Crap. No, I am not cursing; I had a little accident in my pants and am just trying to describe what was now in my briefs.

The next memory I have of that fateful day is that I was bent over Miss Brown's desk, getting whacked four times with a bat that had the inscription, "I need thee every hour." After the spanking, she sent me to my seat to sit down and learn my times table, but I could not. Sit down, that is. But I did learn my times table.

My little brother Tommy was also a student at the school with Miss Brown for about two months. One day, he got into trouble, got spanked, and immediately threw up his lunch. The next week, he was transferred to a school with a principal named Miss Gentles. She did not believe in corporal punishment. I remained at the Miss Brown's school with the other prisoners. I guess when they beat me,

I didn't throw up, and that meant I could handle more beatings. Basically, my digestion issue was at the wrong end.

I am not sure how the spankings I received as a child affected me, but they certainly did not get me to take school seriously. I clowned around most of my school life, managing to learn some things by accident. But every day, my imagination got a good workout, and to this day, I am more likely to be daydreaming than listening to someone's lecture. This is how I have come up with most of my good ideas. Thank God for bad lectures.

Much of the time, as I sat in class, I would reflect on people that I admired and wanted to emulate. Funny people like Charlie Chaplin, the Three Stooges, Jerry Lewis, Abbot and Costello. Every Saturday at 10:00 a.m., my brother and I would attend the movie matinee at a local theater and watch a double feature that usually included a slapstick comedy. To watch Jerry Lewis screw something up and make those faces where his eyes crossed and his mouth squished in made me hysterical. When Charlie Chaplin was chased by the cops and he made that turn where he was on one foot, but the momentum took him wide of his turn – I was in stitches. When Costello had a monster behind him but didn't realize it, and finally turned around and did that double take, I would giggle violently. Laughter was like a drug for me with no bad side effects and no lasting damage.

The first time I went to the circus, I was overwhelmed. It was so big. The three circus tents pointed to the sky like huge castles, and everywhere I looked, there was something magnificent to see. The smell of cotton candy, popcorn, and roasted peanuts blended together, forming its own intoxicating fragrance. When we sat down in the bleachers, I felt like giggling even though nothing was happening. It just felt funny. The colors all around were vibrant and cartoonish, and the stage was set with props I knew would soon come alive with animals, jugglers, and clowns of every shape and size. It was as if I had entered an alternate world where making children happy was the sole purpose, and adults were there to pay for it all. I sat beside my baby brother, and we shared a night of fun so memorable that it imprinted on my mind like a tattoo. At one point, a tiny clown walked around the stage, shaking his butt at the audience and shouting out – "Coca Coooola!" For years, my brother and I mimicked that clown's routine, shaking our buns and shouting out "Coca Coooola!"

The circus is a place of wonder and excitement, especially for six-year-olds. Seeing a stream of endless clowns jumping out of a car the size of my bathtub was beyond hilarious. When the clown with the mop turned around and hit the one with the plunger, he went flying into the one who was peering into an open toilet, who then fell in; this sent signals to my brain that triggered an uncontrollable set of audible responses. Our stomachs hurt so much that we had to try to stop laughing by not watching. From that night on, I was addicted to laughing. I wanted more. I was a laugh junkie.

I can imagine an older kid on the street in a back alley somewhere whispering to me, "Hey, you wanna hear some jokes?" and getting me to follow him to his apartment, where he would have me doing his errands in exchange for jokes he gave on an hourly basis. Then, if I didn't do what he told me, he would withhold the jokes and leave me in a shivering pile on the street, begging strangers to make me laugh. "Please, somebody, give me a joke. It's been thirty minutes since I have had my last laugh."

The good news is that laughing has no such side effects and I will never become enslaved to anyone in exchange for jokes. Even if one laughs all day, no one has ever died laughing. Although I must admit, there was this one day back in 1970 that I did think I would expire due to a serious case of the giggles.

I Almost Died Laughing

Every day, my mom took an afternoon nap. She did this religiously, and everyone in the house knew not to disturb her at this time. If the Pope called during her one hour of beauty rest, we were to take a message. On this particular day, I somehow convinced my mom that I too was tired and needed to sleep for an hour. She agreed to this arrangement, and I got my little brother in on the deal. I was twelve and my brother eight, still young enough to get spanked by my mom, although by this time, I had learned that I could outrun her.

The room in which my mom took a nap had air conditioning, while the rest of the house was unbearably hot. My brother and I would lay on the floor on a mattress at the foot of her bed. Mom closed all the windows and pulled a pillow so tightly over her face that she looked like she would suffocate.

Tommy and I were fully awake. The atmosphere in the room was charged with excitement. We had no intention of sleeping. The stage was set, and now we just waited for the first reason to laugh – my mom's pig-like snoring. Sngggg pcewwwwww. Her two-pronged breathing was like an immediate trigger for the most uncontrolled laughter I have ever experienced. What made this absolutely hysterical was that we had been told not to make a sound under any circumstances. We were under threat of getting thrown out and even spanked with her slipper. The same one she used to crush startled roaches. Have you ever tried not to laugh when told you would be in trouble if you did? It's impossible. The higher the threat of punishment, the more you will giggle.

"You boys need to be quiet. I don't want to hear a peep out of you," my mom ordered as the first sound of muffled laughter escaped from our mouths. There was silence for a few seconds. Then, out of the darkness, you could hear a faint – "Peep." Now, the laughter could be heard in a room across the street.

"Boys, if you cannot be quiet, you are going to have to leave," she insisted with every ounce of seriousness she could muster.

"Okay, Mom," we agreed. Then Tommy and I tried really hard to be absolutely quiet. But now everything was funny. We would sit in the dark, our hands over our mouths, trying desperately not to make a sound, knowing that it was only a matter of time before someone did or said something funny. The next 10 – 15 minutes would be a combination of snoring, snickering, threats, more laughter, promises to be quiet, and the eventual banishment from the bedroom.

Have you ever caught a case of the giggles? I can tell you it's extremely contagious and potentially deadly. The more I laughed, the more my brother laughed. Soon, we were both hyper-ventilating, holding our stomachs, tears welling up in our eyes, and clearly about to die. It was that day that I understood what people meant by 'die laughing.'

It was one of the best times I can remember as a kid, and it didn't cost a dime. Free entertainment courtesy of the Carrington Boys' Entertainment Corp. I am convinced if my brother and I had video games or cable TV, we would never have discovered 'trying to be quiet during mom's nap time.' My brother and I decided that we should try to repeat this activity as often as possible. However, it did become increasingly more difficult to get into my mom's afternoon nap room. She eventually caught on to the fact that we had no intention whatsoever of actually sleeping, and the banishments came as soon as someone giggled.

I learned a lot about being funny as a kid, especially with family members to practice on. The snickering in the room scenario has enhanced my sense of comedy timing to this day. When I do a show for kids, I often tell them they are not allowed to laugh at me, explaining that my show is a serious magic show. This, of course, will raise the odds that they will indeed be laughing at me. Then I pretend to be annoyed, saying, "Hey, cut that out." And asking, "Were you laughing at me?"

It has occurred to me that my parents planned my younger brother's birth in part to provide me a built-in friend. After all, we didn't have TV or the internet at the time, so what was I supposed to do all day – play with myself? That would come later after puberty kicked in.

As children, my brother and I learned to create our own fun, like when we pretended to be newscasters reading the news. I would set up a desk and two chairs and place my five-year-old brother Tommy in front of a make-believe camera – usually a tennis racket tied to a stick and stuck in the ground.

"Hi, welcome to the 6 o'clock news. I am Ronnie Carrington. Now for the headlines. Humpty Dumpty fell off a wall today, and all the King's horses and all the King's men could not put him back together again." Then things would get even more silly.

"In other news, man has finally walked on the moon and will now, along with the cow, attempt to jump over it. We now go live to our on-location Co-Anchor, Tommy Carrington –Tommy."

"Thank you, Ronnie – Three blind mice were reported missing and running around. It seems that the farmer's wife cut off their tails with a carving knife and is now under arrest for the attempted murder of the three special needs animals."

Another activity we invented was a round table discussion about the conditions in our home and around the world. First, I would gather a small committee of people, usually my little brother, the lawn man, and maybe a neighborhood friend or two. Then, we would discuss the serious problems we were facing in the world. Problems like one brother borrowing another brother's socks without first asking for permission. This would trigger a thirty-minute debate worthy of CNN's Meet the Press. In the end, solving the Carrington brothers' sock dilemma proved as elusive as solving world hunger. My younger brother would insist he was not lending me any of his posessions and that I should just get my own socks. I would argue that all his things were really mine in the first place since they were hand-me-downs, and he should just hand me back what I needed. If he refused, I would threaten to sneak into his room and steal them during the night. Then Tommy would promise to retaliate by telling my mom. Now I would have to declare war, and my first mission would be to hide his blanket – the one he walked around with all day pressed to his lips while he puckered his mouth. My mom would call it his security blanket, so he must have felt it would protect him somehow. I would tape these round table discussions with my Sony Cassette Recorder and play them back later for further analysis.

All these make-believe round table discussions were great fun and probably helped us work out some of our real-life disputes. Even as I write this, I am keenly aware that, as brothers, we will always have issues. Sometimes, we still act like children and refuse to talk to each other. It's too bad we are not nearly as good at working out our problems as adults, as we were when we were kids. I believe my brother and I need to spend some time on a mattress at the foot of my mom's bed during her afternoon rest time. It would place us on the same side and in opposition to our mom, who is, quite frankly, the source of many of our conflicts. Thirty minutes of giggling would go a long way in helping us put things in perspective. Just

two brothers defying their mother's instructions and having a hell of
a lot of fun doing so.

Daddy Lectures

As a kid, I was always in awe of my father's work ethic, discipline, posture, auto repair knowledge and organizational skills. He just had his shit together. One example of my dad's high-level managerial skills was the 'spare-item-closet' in which he stored items we as a family might need. Almost every day, someone in the house needed something that could not be found, and my dad would have a 'spare-whatever' in his locked closet. "Anybody know where I can find a pair of scissors?" my mother might yell out. Then, we would all start looking for the pair of scissors that were supposed to be in the 'scissors draw.' Of course, no one could find them. But we all knew who would be able to produce a pair.

"Mom needs a pair of scissors," I would tell Dad. Then, he would go into his pre-getting-the-requested-item-routine.

"I keep telling you all to put the scissors back in the scissors drawer when you are finished with them, but none of you will listen. Now you want me to lend you my scissors? I am not giving you my scissors. You know you are not going to give them back to me when you're finished."

That was the introduction to a 10-minute lecture on why we should all be more organized. Nobody was listening. We just waited for the speech to be over so we could get the damn scissors. I remember trying to peek inside his secret closet when he would open it to get the requested item and be captivated by what I saw. If only I could get a hold of those keys; I could get my hands on some really cool stuff.

On the days my dad was in a good mood, we would ask him if

we could get a soda. We never had sodas in our refrigerator. They were considered a non-essential luxury while owning a genuine antique Queen Elizabeth pineapple-crusted mahogany dining room table[8] was considered necessary. But we knew Dad had sodas in his secret closet. He would produce them when guests would come over, or my mom wanted one. This request almost always inspired a different lecture than the one for scissors. The first part of this lecture was an explanation of why he was not going to give us any sodas, and it was delivered while he would get the keys to the closet, open it, and hand us each a soda.

"I keep telling you kids that sodas are bad for you, and you should all be drinking water. Here, take this Pepsi to your mom. Sodas are full of sugar and chemicals; you are going to grow up addicted to sugar. Here, give this orange soda to Tommy. I will not contribute to your bad habits by giving you sodas to drink when there are healthier, cheaper alternatives. Here, Ronnie, this pineapple soda is for you." We would just endure the speech and run off with the sodas.

One day, my dad went to work and left an extra pair of keys to the inner sanctum by his bedside. I knew it was strictly prohibited to go into his forbidden space, but I couldn't help myself. I opened the closet, and a smell that was unique to this one spot in the universe hit me in the face and forced me to think of my dad. It was as if he was there. I had smelled that distinct combination of Old Spice aftershave mixed with my dad's natural odors coming from that closet, but usually, he would have been standing in front of it, carefully handing me the requested items and blocking my view from all the goodies. But here I stood, mesmerized by the variety of items that lay before me like a miniature convenience store on steroids, and no one to stop me from checking it all out. The shelves

---

[8] My mother was an antique collector and dealer for years, so she had good reason to have expensive antique furniture in our home.

were packed with every item one could imagine. There were packs of hand soap, razor blades, deodorant, shaving lotion, masking tape, Christmas wrapping paper, rope, string, washcloths, snacks, books, magazines, and extra rolls of toilet paper. And that was the bottom shelf. Then I saw some of the forbidden items. His one–of–a–kind mirror was rigged with wire so he could wrap it around his head and cut his own hair. His collection of 8 track tapes and LP records with singers like Bing Cosby, Tennessee Ernie Ford, Perry Como, Dean Martin, and others nobody under 60 would recognize. And most forbidden of all – boxes of beer and cigarettes by the carton. I took a soda and locked the door. I knew there was a good chance that Dad would know someone took a soda, but I was hoping it was a small enough infraction not to necessitate an all-out investigation.

It was a genius plan. Dad had devised a way to teach us children life lessons. Over several years, he had managed to lecture us about good hygiene when we needed toothpaste, healthy eating habits when someone wanted cookies, returning items to their "home" when we needed scissors, and why we should never smoke when mom needed cigarettes. The problem was by the time I became an adult, I had poor dental habits, ate poorly, was extremely disorganized and smoked. So much for his lectures.

As tough as my dad was on me when it came to not fooling around, I always saw him as someone who gave his best effort to being a father and husband. He never shied away from his responsibility to bring up his children with a healthy dose of 'broughtupsy.' And Dad was not just about preaching to us. He lived what he preached. He ate right, exercised, didn't drink sodas, didn't smoke, got up early, worked hard, walked with his shoulders upright and his feet straight, brushed his teeth several times daily and spoke proper English. To this day, every time I say the word 'ask' I make sure to annunciate the k so that it doesn't sound like 'ass' because I remember when I would say, "Dad, can I ass you something?" he would tell me that an ass was a donkey. Don't 'ass' me why I remember that.

Even though my dad's insistence that I learn to repair an automobile was met with great resistance, I knew he was just trying to pass down his valuable know-how to his son. He was proud of his ability to make his 10-year-old Oldsmobile Cutlass run like it had just come off the factory assembly line.

"Do you hear that?" he would ask when driving to school at 25 mph. "Hear what?" I would respond.

"Exactly. You can't hear a thing. The rattle in the right of the front chassis is gone. I tightened the frame, repaired the drum brakes, and reset the timing." It was like he was speaking another language.

"Yeah, sure, sounds good. Dad, could you speed up? You are going 25 mph in a 50 mph zone."

"Feel how smooth the transmission changes gears? I had to rebuild the transmission. Took me all night. Your mother won't notice all the work I've done, but somebody should appreciate it."

"Dad, why have you slowed down to 15 mph? I'm going to be late for school," I would reason. Then he would step on the accelerator, flooding the huge V8 engine with gas, reaching speeds in excess of 70 mph in mere seconds. Dad only drove his cars at two speeds. Too slow or too fast. I didn't like either one.

"Dad, do you mind slowing down a bit? I'm feeling really nervous."

"I know what I am doing," he would snap.[9] "Just relax."

I would try really hard, but I couldn't relax. Especially when he would overtake a car, and we were heading directly toward a truck at breakneck speed. Then at the last possible moment, he would swerve back into the proper lane, and I would think, "Damn, he does know what he's doing."

At night Dad would be under his car, tightening some screw, bleeding the brakes, or doing an engine overhaul. Occasionally, I would be recruited to help. He would place me in the vehicle, and then start barking orders.

"PRESS THE BRAKES ALL THE WAY TO THE FLOOR. HEY, ALL THE WAY TO THE FLOOR! STOP! NOT THAT FAR. WHAT ARE YOU DOING? – PUMP THE BRAKES! HARDER! NOT SO HARD! THAT'S ENOUGH! HARDER! PUMP THE BRAKES!"

I usually quit before the job was finished. I couldn't take the snapping.

"Dad, I have homework to do, sorry, gotta go. Get Tommy to pump the brakes." Then, as I left, I would hear how someday I was going to wish I had learned how to replace the brakes, spark plugs, or timing belts on my car and save myself thousands of dollars.

I can honestly say my dad was completely wrong on this one. Not once in my sixty-plus years of life have I paid for a car repair and wished I had saved the money by doing it myself. Especially when I watch the mechanics hook up my car to a $50,000 computer, diagnose the problem like they were diagnosing a human being with

---

[9] Snap, derived from Snapper – This is when Dad would talk in a manner that would make the listener feel bitten.

heart disease, and then perform a procedure that would rival triple bypass surgery in complexity. I did try to change the oil in my car once. But when my dad saw me with $25 worth of oil and filters under the car, looking for the thing-a-ma-jig that lets the oil out, he suggested I pay the $19.99 for an oil change. He finally realized I wasn't cut out for this work-on-motorcar thing.

Dad was by far the bravest man I ever knew. When I was 12 years old, he was diagnosed with kidney stones and had to go to the hospital to await their passing. If the kidney stones didn't pass on their own, the surgeons would go in and get 'em. The day he was to be admitted, I gave him the horn from my bicycle and told him it was something he could squeeze if he felt pain. He took the horn and seemed to appreciate my gesture of goodwill, squeezing it as he got into the car and all the way out of our driveway.

It was July of 1971. I had a summer job a few miles from the hospital where Dad lay in a bed waiting for the stones to exit his body. For a twelve-year-old, this was a horrifying idea. A stone passing through a man's penis? The math didn't seem to add up. I had never seen a stone I thought could travel through that small of a channel. When I was told it was a painful experience, it didn't take much explanation for me to concur.

Almost every day, I would leave my job working as a bag boy for a local retail store and stop by the hospital to visit my dad. When he saw me approaching his room, he would reach under the sheets, pull out the bike horn, and begin squeezing it like it was a New Year's Eve celebration.

"Look who's here!" he would say with a smile that clearly took great effort to produce. I would stand at the edge of his bed, wishing I could make the bad kidney stones disappear and watching as the nurses came to his room with pain medication. I remember how he would refuse the medication on the principle that the more pills he took, the less effective the meds would become. Instead, he would attempt to grin and bear it. When he did take the drugs, it didn't seem to help much anyway. But I never heard my dad complain of pain. If it wasn't for his face, I would never have known he was suffering.

I cannot recall many words being exchanged between my father and me on those visits, but I recall feeling like he appreciated my company, due in part to the constant horn-blowing that took place. That summer, I felt closer to my dad than I had at any time I can remember. It would not be long before we would drift apart, and our very different ways of thinking pushed me toward the comfort of my mother's worldview, which included an allowance for academic mediocrity and lots of fooling around. I am sure that was not her intention. I was determined that my teenage years would be filled with gallivanting while my dad was intent on getting me ready to take life seriously. On the contrary, it seemed that my mother was more likely to appreciate my cause and lobby to give me more freedom. So, I recruited her in my fight against my dad's rules. In return, I empathized with her sentiment that my father was both unreasonable and humorless. She, in turn, rated me as the favorite among her children. And her rating system was often well publicized. Being number one was the worst thing that could have happened to me. First, this situation did not endear me to any of my siblings, and I was just one coat of many colors away from being sold into slavery. Ultimately, I missed out on many of the valuable life lessons my father was trying to teach me since I had such strong support from his female counterpart. And as it turns out, sometimes support for our plans can help us get our own way and really screw us up.

If I was the kid who was always fooling around, my dad was the father who would put a stop to it. This often placed us at opposite ends of a how-to-approach life philosophy. I thought it was quite acceptable to make fun of the preacher's bald head at church, and Dad thought I should listen to the sermon. I wanted to crack jokes at dinner time, and he wanted me to eat my supper. I lived to clown around, and he seemed unable to take a break from his way-too-serious life.

One day, my dad gave my little brother an order to pick up his shoes from the front porch, and I stood behind him, mimicking his order. I was trying to make my brother laugh. When my dad realized I was behind him making fun of a serious situation, he turned around, slapped me across my face, and said, "Don't you dare make fun of me." Then he walked off and left me standing in front of my audience with absolutely nowhere to go with this routine. My face hurt a lot less than my ego. I guess making fun of Dad needed to be eliminated from my repertoire. I had not realized that my clowning around could lead to such complete humiliation, and over time, I would learn that one man's joke could end up being another man's reason to take offense. Humor is a risky business, and life as a clown is not always so damn funny. It was probably necessary for me to experience a slap in the face at the end of a punch line. It woke me up to the reality that jokes can backfire. Maybe that's why they call it slapstick comedy. I'm just glad that with the slap, there wasn't a stick. To be fair to my father, I must admit I do understand how he would see my mimicking him as disrespectful, and the next time I was tempted to mimic his behavior – I made a mental note to duck.

Music To My Ears

Some of my earliest memories of living on this earth involved my dad, music, and the smell of reel-to-reel tapes packed neatly on a custom-made shelf in his special music room. I don't remember my mother ever being in this room. My guess is she really would have preferred to have transformed that space into a bedroom, tearoom, storage room, or knitting room. Anything other than what it had become. But Dad had captured this small space, marked it like an animal in the jungle, and held on to it till he no longer had a say in what happened to the real estate within his own castle.

Space, in any home, is of prime value, and the struggle to claim that space has been a source of conflict between partners from the beginning of time. Getting your partner to agree to place a pool table in the den could potentially end up being the equivalent of getting Pharaoh to let your people go. It may take several plagues to acquire some type of concession. Even when my father worked hard and earned a good living, my mother would often point out several important reasons why the space Dad wanted for his personal projects would be better used if open to the entire tribe. How my father carved out an 8-by-10-foot room to house his prized reel-to-reel tape recorder, a pull-out single bed, and the only air conditioner in the entire house is still a mystery to me. But in 1965, when I was only six years old and fresh off my Chevy-destroying, rock-throwing debacle, I spent time with Dad in his private sanctuary, listening to songs like Perry Como's "Catch a Falling Star" and feeling a kinship with my father that was clearly related to our mutual love for the experience.

The wide selection of music that Dad had acquired would rival almost any teenager's music playlist. The songs were analogous to the life he lived and the things he held dear, especially in relation to the many paths love can take us on. When Jim Reeves sang, "Put your sweet lips a little closer to the phone, let's pretend we're here together all alone," I imagined he was telling this to my mom. The music was representative of both my father's sentimental disposition and his desire to express his romantic passions.

Dad and I sat for hours breathing in the sweet sounds and singing along with Bing Crosby, Nat King Cole, Tennessee Ernie Ford, and other memorable voices. The songs would stick in my head so firmly that I would sing them in the shower or whistle the tune all night. Sometimes the song would refuse to stop playing in my head and felt like it was attached to my brain with crazy glue. The music took us away from the tedium of life and stirred up emotions that had previously sat dormant.

When Dad played Jimmy Dean singing Big Bad John, I thought the story about a big man who gave his life to save others trapped in a coal mine was about my dad. His first name, after all, was John, and Dad was certainly big and bad. When Tennessee Ernie Ford sang a gospel song, his deep bass voice made me feel like God was speaking. Then I remember feeling really sad that Tom Dooley would have to hang down his head. The poor boy was going to die. The song about the blizzard where the man was only 100 yards away from safety still gives me goosebumps, and I am still wondering who the exotic woman with the Spanish eyes was, although I did know she lived down Mexico Way.

Ultimately, I learned a lot about love and life from the music my father played. For example, I learned that a woman was like a lemon tree: very pretty, but the fruit was impossible to eat. And having tried to eat the fruit of love, I will tell you that even if you can eat a lemon, it often leaves you bitter.

I also learned that everybody loves somebody sometimes and that some women, like certain songs, were unforgettable. Eventually, Dad took his music on the road in the form of 8-track tapes. I remember this new high-tech medium as such a step up from records and reel-to-reel tapes. After all, I could hit a button and jump to the middle of a completely arbitrary song.

When we moved from the house where Dad had his music room, it seemed my father was no longer able to pull off his capture house space trick, except for the small cupboard I described in the previous chapter. My mother had by then captured all the indoor space and kept her soon-to-be restored antique furniture in all the extra rooms. The items would fill the rooms, leaving only a small corridor that led to a bed my mom used on occasion to get her afternoon nap. The house had no room for music and barely enough room for my dad.

When my dad was in the later stages of his life, he didn't even have a closet. Everything he held dear, including his music, was kept in the trunk of his 1981 Chevy Monte Carlo. It was quite common to see him standing behind his car, the trunk open, scrounging through the last space on earth he could control, trying to find a tape to play in his automobile. He may not have had much left, but he still had his music.

The Trouble With School

On my first day of high school, Larry Dixon and Bobby Miller greeted me with pretend merriment as I walked to my new classroom. At first, I was suspicious of their desire to talk to me since they were both seniors and I, being a freshman, was not someone with whom young men would want to associate. They asked me questions regarding how I felt about being in high school, and I thought they were being kind to a kid who was terrified. But schoolboys, being the sinister creatures they are, are prone to harass those who are vulnerable. And so, as Larry spoke with me, Bobby placed a unique type of shrub up the bottom of my pants, and then they both waited for me to walk off. The shrub was a plant that schoolboys had discovered would crawl up the inside of a person's pants until it stuck them in the crotch. As long as the person walked, the plant would move up. It took me about six steps to realize what these two 'friends' had done to me. By then, the bush had crawled up far enough that removing it would require me placing a hand down my pants. This was sure to give them, and the crowd that would gather, a good laugh.

I faced a dilemma. Stop right in front of them, reach down, and attempt to locate the item, thereby providing the show these two scums were hoping for. Or keep walking like nothing was wrong while anticipating the eventual meeting of the now itchy bush with my balls. I chose plan B and had to walk a hundred yards or so to the nearest restroom, acting as if all was right with the world, while the bush attacked my privates.

Once I reached puberty, something disturbing kicked in. I believe the technical term is 'stupidity.' I went from being a relatively compliant child to a kid determined to break many of the rules established by my parents and teachers. I cannot say I understand why this happened. I just know that when the term 'teen' was added to my description, along with a large dose of testosterone, it triggered a desire to experiment with activities that could kill me. Smoking in the boy's room at school, drinking a whole six-pack of beer, and riding a motorcycle at reckless speeds. Often all during the same time frame. This stage of my life was the starting point for a heightened battle with my father that would continue until I met the next mature figure in my life – my wife. My dad, like my wife, did not approve of immature, juvenile, destructive, selfish, or self-centered behavior, and both would end up loving me enough to demand a better version of myself.

But when I was thirteen, I had not yet met my wife. So Dad was on his own. Dad spent much time racking his brain to find solutions to my defiance, which started with my constant 'partying' and resulted in my disinterest in school. And believe me when I tell you that I hated school and thought all my teachers should be fired for 'excessive boringness.' My history teacher wanted us to remember dates for god's sake. What in the world for? Why did I need to know that in 1536, King Henry VIII of England had his wife Anne beheaded? I did find it interesting that he beheaded the poor woman as opposed to divorcing her.

What I was interested in was riding my motorcycle, visiting my girlfriends, going to dance parties, drinking beer, skipping school, and, on occasion, driving my mom's 68 Buick Skylark around town at high speeds without her knowledge. I admit now that these life choices were probably not the best, but they were, in my opinion, quite understandable under the circumstances.

What were the circumstances? A lot of sub-par high school teachers, a selection of immature friends, a very active imagination, and a Yamaha motorcycle sitting in my house. How could my dad bring home such a distraction and expect me not to be…well…distracted? No doubt, I had a form of ADD, which led to my inability to add. Or subtract.

One day in Biology class, my teacher, Miss Gorden, was talking about small, microscopic bacteria known as an Amoeba when things got really ugly. I happened to be daydreaming, my favorite hobby, when I heard the teacher say my name in connection with a question. I remember the question very clearly because of what happened next. The teacher explained that the Amoeba can form arm-like structures called pseudopodia, which it uses to engulf food, or something to that effect. When she looked in my direction and saw that I was the only kid in the class who was not paying attention, she called out my name.

"Carrington, what is the name of an Amoeba's arm-like structures used to engulf food?" she asked. All 35 kids in the class stared at me. She had just moments before explained this very phenomenon, so the answer to everyone in the class was very clear.

"The Amoeba, eating food. Carrington, were you listening?" she asked.

"No," I said timidly, all the while sinking lower in my chair. The class erupted in laughter, only I had not told a joke. The teacher turned to the class and repeated the question. The students, in unison, like a choir singing a song, shouted out the answer.

"Pseudopodia, Miss Gorden." Now, if that was all that happened, it would have been just another day at school. But for reasons outside of my understanding, the boys in the class decided that they had just discovered the perfect nickname for their classmate. They were no longer going to call me Carrington, Ronnie, or even my previous nickname, Gilligan. (after Gilligan on Gilligan's Islands).

Any of these names would have been fine with me. But Pseudopodia? This was a direct reminder of my daydreaming in class and my failure to answer a question that every other kid could answer. For the next three years of my high school life, I would be referred to as Pseudopodia. Or Pseudo for short. No amount of complaining was going to change that. It would define me as a boy who was snickered at, ridiculed and shunned. I was the dumbest kid in a class of bright kids. From that day on, I hated my classmates, I hated my teachers, I hated my school, and just maybe, I hated myself.

It was a difficult stage for me. The audience, filled with my peers and teachers, was unforgiving, and my performances, unappreciated. In the end, I just wanted to get out of school as soon as possible and move on to bigger and better things. But college, as it turns out, was smaller and worse.

Brotherly Rumble

Unlike my younger brother, who was athletically challenged and consequently elected to refrain from anything more physically demanding than jogging, my older brother Richard was athletically obsessed. As soon as I was old enough, he challenged me to several physical contests that would establish his superiority as a human being.

The first challenge came when I was ten years old. He was eighteen, and we foot-raced down the street in front of our house. I was left behind in a cloud of dust. It would not have made a difference if we were both the same age. He was fast. Running was something he had perfected during his high school years where he held several track records at 440 and 880 yards for many years and enjoyed telling everyone who would listen all about it. When I was twelve, he proposed that we settle on who could jump further from a standing position, and after much psyching himself up, Richard managed to jump at least two inches further than me. Sometimes Richard would suggest some type of random competition that we would both take so seriously one would think it was an Olympic event, and this led to several heavily contested bouts of 'let's see who can hit the tennis ball off the wall in the living room filled with mom's antique vases the most amount of times, without the ball hitting the ground, or any vases.' The record was twenty-eight times with only one broken China cup and one slightly chipped vase. I contend my brother holds the record and is responsible for the damage.

So here we had two brothers with years of pent-up resentment and animosity, determined to establish their physical superiority, jacked up on testosterone, and relishing the chance to beat the shit out of each other until someone gave up or Mom and Dad stopped the slaughter. Except on this occasion, Mom and Dad were not around.

I was now 15 years old, 5 foot 10 inches, and weighing in at 145 lbs. and my brother was 24 years old, 5 foot 10 inches, and weighing in at about 165 lbs. What I lacked in weight, I made up for in coordination and speed. Or that was my theory, at least. By this time in our athletic careers, we had fought close battles in several sports, including but not limited to: one on one soccer, tennis, table tennis, standing long-jump, push-ups, arm-wrestling, pull-ups, holding our breath, sprinting, getting Mom's attention, and debate. I, by virtue of a healthy dose of athleticism, had established myself as a worthy challenger in every activity. But now we were entering an entirely new arena. This was not a sport where the winner was determined by hitting a tennis ball harder. The hitting that would take place would be to someone's face and would involve significant pain, which we were both happy to dish out.

Richard and I put on boxing gloves. We agreed to a few vague rules like 'when hitting below the belt, allow time for the opponent's balls to fall back into place.'

Then we went at it, throwing a barrage of wild punches with everything we had. There were several left jabs for all the jabs spoken around the dinner table. A right uppercut for the times he had cut me down in front of Dad. The flurry must have lasted at least sixty seconds. If you have ever boxed, you will know that one needs to be supremely fit to engage in this type of activity for several three-minute rounds. After sixty seconds, a novice will find that no matter how much willpower they possess, their hands will no longer cooperate with their brain and will refuse to be raised above waist level. Punching at that point is absolutely out of the question. I remember feeling like my arms were filled with lead and my body was in a laundry machine that cycled through a wash-and-spin dry before I had time to reset to gentle.

I punched and was punched enough to know that boxing should be considered cruel and unusual punishment and that calling this a sport was like calling passing kidney stones a hobby. I cannot say with any accuracy who won the three sixty-second bouts since I was busy trying not to die at the time. But I believe my brother would agree we could call it a draw since both of us had been hit enough to last us a lifetime, and we just wanted to go somewhere private to lick our emotional wounds. I must add that I was only fifteen at the time and still developing. In other words, if we were to have a rematch at the present time – neither of us could box for more than ten seconds, and both of us know better than to try.

Ultimately, I believe that anyone who has an older brother is required by the universe to have at least one major confrontation with their older sibling so that pecking order guidelines can be readjusted. Otherwise, the older brother would just push you around till one of you is dead.

I must add that it was truly amazing how little we argued during our competitions.

Somehow, we played fair and trusted each other completely. For example, when playing tennis, if I called his ball out, he would accept my call without much questioning.[10] And vice versa.

In contrast to our civility in the athletic arena, we were literally at each other's throats when it came to who would get the last piece

---

[10] A short exchange of words may occur, including "Are you sure?" (allowed one time), "It looked in to me," (allowed one time), and "You lying piece of shit" (whispered under one's breath repeatedly).

of chicken from the dinner table or who the Dean Martin records he had taken from my dad's "special closet" belonged to. Maybe the sporting events gave us a healthier option for getting rid of pent-up hostility, which gives me an idea. I need to call him up and challenge him to some type of physical challenge. Maybe see who can still tie their shoes without sitting down.

Sister Secrets

Rosie spent more than eight months of each of her final few years of high school away at an all-girls' boarding school. I remember my parents discussing what to do with her once the natural attraction to boys caused her Christian upbringing to weaken, and her determination to hang out with members of the opposite sex unsupervised drove her to several unsanctioned secret rendezvous. All I knew was there were some very handsome older boys who had attempted to hang out with my fourteen-year-old sister. I think they planned on holding hands, maybe even kissing. Being only eight at the time, I was never fully informed as to the details of the questionable activities. However, I have since learned that she was spotted at a location outside of the school she should have been attending. Soon after being caught, Rosie was shipped off to an all-girls' boarding school in the mountains far away for the naughty boys. I remember going to visit her while she was doing her time, and I really enjoyed those visits. Never in my life have I ever had so much attention from so many of the opposite sex. Hundreds of high school girls, who seemed to be boy-deprived, started peeking out of classrooms, dorm windows, and hallways at the 12-year-old boy who walked around the school grounds. Some of them would send messages via my sister saying how cute they thought I was, and others would send me notes asking me about my life or expressing a desire to meet me. One such young lady was Mary, who was also twelve years old at the time and, as such, was way more mature than me and really out of my league. If I had met this same young lady when I was twenty, the gap would have been much closer, but at twelve, I was a giggling bundle of boyishness, and she was a lady. But I remember her sending word to me that she thought I was handsome, and when I saw her adorably skinny little female body, I fell in love. It was a feeling that only one year prior I would not have had, and in fact, the idea of flirting with a girl when I was eleven would have been downright sickening.

Sometime later, my sister started dating Mary's brother, David, and I got to go with her, her boyfriend, and Mary on a double date to a restaurant. This was to be my first date ever, though in reality, I was sent by my Mom to keep an eye on my sister. The small rustic restaurant had a jukebox, and I recall sitting across from Mary for a very long time, psyching myself up to the point where I would have the courage to ask her to slow dance. I was thinking this would put Mary and me in close proximity and expose me to emotions I had wanted to experience for at least the previous two months. Loving a woman, after all, was a good thing, and it was about time I learned how to handle touching one. Finally, I was ready to pop the question and accept my fate, and I proposed to Mary that we dance together. She said yes, and that is when I started to worry about stepping on her toes and tripping her during our slow dance. I placed a dime in the jukebox and chose the song we would dance to. Red Red Wine by Neil Diamond. We fumbled through several possible ways of holding hands till we accidentally ended up looking like Fred Astaire and Ginger Rogers with my left hand on her shoulder and the other hand neatly fitting into hers. Holding this attractive twelve-year-old close to my body was better than anything I had ever experienced up to that point in all my years on Earth, and it was the first time I realized I wanted to have one of them to call my own. If I had been allowed to marry Mary, I would have, but my parents probably wouldn't have allowed me to bring her home since all my sleepover friends had to be boys. And even if they did allow her to come home with me, they most certainly would not have allowed her to sleep in my bed. I have no idea why not. I just wanted to cuddle with her. That night I contemplated giving Mary a kiss on the lips, but I was too scared of screwing this up. It would be at least another year before I would gain the courage to get that physical, and by then, Mary and I had gone our separate ways.

Sometimes, Dad would visit Rosie at the boarding school, and he would come home with stories of how she played the guitar and sang songs that brought him to tears. Dad would walk around the house singing, "Goodbye, Daddy, darling, I'll miss you." It was pathetic. How could she reduce this 6-foot-plus man of steel to such a crybaby?

When Rosie would come home from boarding school for the holidays, she would tell me about her friends at school and how they would sneak out at night to visit the young men at the all-boys' boarding school just down the street. They really should have built the boys' school much further away from the girls' school. Surely, they should have known that anything less than fifty miles would not be much of a deterrent to girls who were sent to the school primarily because they were attracted to boys and, even more importantly, were attracting boys. Rosie and her friends would calculate their temporary escape from the locked-down facility for months with Navy Seal-like precision, and her description of how they put pillows under the bed covers to simulate sleeping schoolgirls created tension worthy of a Stephen King novel.

I remember loving the stories of all the things she and her school friends would do that were against the rules. I particularly enjoyed the accounts of how they would sneak in boxes of food that her friends would get from their rich parents and how they would stuff themselves till they were sick and had to puke. Coming from a family in which food was carefully rationed like we were wartime prisoners made these stories seem surreal, and I remember imagining the spread like it was a feast of my favorite foods.

But the best part about this equation was that my big sister trusted me enough to share her little secrets, and I was honored by her level of honesty. I did keep everything she told me close to the vest and am only divulging the info after getting the go-ahead to do so. This stage of our lives was unique in that I was finally old enough to be part of her world, and she was young enough to allow me to be part of hers. But it wouldn't be long before she had finished school and would be dating men, and the stories would be too mature for a young teenager. By then, she was telling her secrets to my older brother, and this, for reasons that will remain secret, was somewhat ill-advised.

Having an older sister taught me a lot about stages in life. At the time, we went to Disney World and took her with us. This sounded like a good idea until you consider she was a seventeen-year-old girl. While my little brother and I were having a ball on the Pirates of the Caribbean ride, she was sulking because she was missing her newest boyfriend. My mom thought she was being terribly selfish and ungrateful, and it wasn't till I had my first steady girlfriend that I realized how horrible it would be to force me to go to visit Mickey Mouse without my steady girlfriend, Debby. This boy-girl thing turns out to be quite a powerful phenomenon, and my parents spent a lot of time and effort trying to manage these powerful forces without sitting us down to explain any of it, although I do admit that much of it is really quite unexplainable.

Pretty Good Parents

John and Gwen were fairly typical parents, which means they didn't have a clue what they were doing. Parenting children is like training a cat to do tricks. The trainer is gonna be frustrated, the cat is going to be annoyed, and nobody is gonna be happy. Like most subjective things in life, teaching your children to live in a way that significantly reduces the chances of having to bail them out of jail someday is more or less a crapshoot. But that doesn't mean that parents should give up trying. At least not until the children have become adults, which is sometime after they turn sixty. Or when they stop hitting up their parents for money. Whichever comes first. My parents utilized the then cutting-edge advice of their generation on how to bring up children. The Guru was known as Dr. Spock. But it didn't stop me from reckless behavior.

One day, when I was about fourteen years old, I had the bright idea to borrow the keys to my parents' sixty-eight Buick Skylark and take it for a spin.[11] I had a clue how to drive but not the legal documentation. It was about 2:00 a.m. when I had the compulsion to risk everything my parents had worked for on a thirty-minute reckless joy ride. I took the keys from my dad's bedside table, which was two feet from his sleeping body, and tiptoed to the Buick parked in our backyard carport about six inches away from the Oldsmobile. Then I started up the car, slowly drove it down the street, and upon reaching Jacks Hill Road, floored it. This, I must tell you, was a rush. First of all, under the hood was a 455.72-cubic-inch Buick V8 engine rated at 350 hp and capable of speeds in excess of 115 mph. At least that's as fast as I got it to go before I ran out of road. I

---

[11] Spin: Driving the car in a circle, producing smoke and tire tracks.

managed to make it to and from the party I attended in one piece, but the next morning, my dad came into my room to have a little discussion with me.

"I need to talk to you about last night," he said, pulling up a chair so he could sit near my bed.

I tried to look dazed and confused as I sat up in the bed, wiping my eyes and yawning.

"What about last night?"

"I know you took the car out."

I quickly discerned a tone of confidence and immediately knew I should shut my mouth. He continued.

"When I parked the Buick, it was three inches from the Oldsmobile. This morning, I noticed the two cars were six inches from each other."

You measure the distance of the parked cars? I thought to myself.

"Someone moved the car, and it wasn't your mother."

I tried to think of anyone else in the family I could pin this 'car movement' on, but I knew my younger brother Tommy, the only other sibling living with us at the time, would never have done such a risky thing, at least not since the rock throwing incident. I remained speechless and waited for my punishment, which I was hoping would not leave permanent scars.

"You drove the car last night, correct?"

He was going to make me confess. I was terrified. My dad had always been a no-nonsense man. When it came to discipline, he was not weak or shy. I was thinking no TV, no parties, no friends over for years. And maybe something even more radical, like forcing me to eat dinner the nights my mom served cow tongue or eggplant. But Dad took a surprising turn. He opted for one of his lectures.

"Everything your mother and I have worked so hard to provide our family with could be all lost in a matter of seconds if your irresponsible behavior resulted in someone being injured or killed," he started. "An underage, unlicensed, uninsured driver whose actions caused property damage or injury could easily result in a lawsuit. Why would you risk all of that for a moment of pleasure?"

This was an excellent question for which I had no answer. I felt sick as if I needed to bring up the breakfast I had not yet eaten. My dad's lecture was reacting poorly with my hangover. I nodded in acknowledgment of my dad's logic. It was impacting me in a way I knew would permanently change my future behavior.

"In time," he continued, "you will have a license and a car to drive. Hopefully, by then, you will have learned to drive responsibly. Until then, don't take any more chances." Then he put back the chair and left the room. No punishment, no curfew, no grounding. Just a short lecture that left me shaken to the core. That was the last time I drove a car without a license.

Unfortunately, it was not the last time I would act irresponsibly. But I could cross reckless, youthful, unlicensed driving off my list of crazy things to do.

Storytelling Mom

My mom was not so big on the verbal encouragement. She was much more likely to express her own virtues than those of her children or other people. According to my mom, she thought she was fantastic, and everybody loved her. She was not shy about telling people how good she was at getting along with everybody, having long-term friends, decorating, writing, psychology, parenting, baking, selling, nutrition, and listening. I just listened. She wasn't entirely wrong. Just a tad pretentious.

But Mom was a survivor. Brought up relatively poor, with parents who were constantly fighting each other, she and her brother often went hungry. She learned how to do whatever it took to survive, including manipulating people.

My mom is one of the best storytellers I know. In fact, almost everything she says is really a story of some sort. Some are true, some are fiction. Sometimes, the story is a mixture of truth and fiction integrated in such a way no one can tell the difference. She would have my dad jumping through hoops with her song and dance numbers, and eventually, my dad just followed her directions. He was in awe of her cleverness and acting skills, along with her dyed blond hair and really large boobs.

Mom was so good at making stuff up to suit her needs that she became an expert at catching others when they tried to do the same. Everybody learned it was impossible to lie to Mom. She would lie to catch you in a lie, and that's no lie. Mom has told me thousands of times that she never lies, and apparently, she believes that.

My family has often agreed that my mom could have worked for the CIA because of her ability to extract information, track down her children, discover undercover operations, and get us to talk. As a result, her four children rarely got away with anything underhanded.

One night, when I was fourteen years old, my parents allowed me to go over to my friend Christopher's house to spend the night. My friend was no saint, and he and I disappeared from his house in the wee hours of the night to go over and hang out with Damien, an 18-year-old friend of my friend, with whom my parents would not have wanted me to hang. Damien had his own apartment in which all sorts of sinful behavior took place. At the time, I was open to participating in many types of aberrant activities. I remember Damien's apartment being really cool, with wall-to-wall fluorescent posters of rock stars and partially naked women, creating an atmosphere reminiscent of the hippie movement in the 70s. Come to think of it, this was the 70s, and my friend Damien did have long hair and a hint of societal rebellion. Within a few hours, a small group of teenage boys had gathered to drink rum and cokes, listen to Led Zeppelin records, and smoke cigarettes without the threat of parental interruption. After a few rums and cokes, things began to get a bit fuzzy, but I do recall lying down on one of the hip leather couches in the apartment, looking at the walls and wondering why they were moving. At one point, there was some discussion of getting girls to come to the party, and I wondered if it was really possible to find parents who would allow their daughters to come to a bachelor pad at three in the morning and what we would possibly do with them once they arrived. But before I could find out, my mom pulled one of her 'blue vase'[12] investigations and managed to wake up my friend's parents, have them locate our whereabouts (I am not sure

---

[12] Based on a story of how someone had unwaveringly persevered in a

quest to obtain a blue vase.

how), and have me extracted from the dungeon of iniquity. I was promptly taken home where I was interrogated and sent to my own bed. I have no idea what other inappropriate behavior I would have participated in besides teenage smoking and drinking, but I am of the opinion that it could easily have gotten worse and that this would have further complicated my already rebellious teenage years. I have come to appreciate having parents who tried really hard to keep up with their son's activities as I gain an understanding of the dangers of addictions, poor life choices, and destructive lifestyles. Especially as I realize how significantly this is all related to experiences I had as a teenager when I was so susceptible to making questionable decisions.

Waitering In Vain

After high school, I went to live with my sister for a year in Miami, Florida. She had been married for at least two years, so she was clearly ready to take on the responsibility of dealing with a teenager. While living with my sister, I was able to discover several things I was not very good at while still managing to remain clueless as to what to do with my life. First, I learned that I was prone to locking my keys in my car, losing my wallet, and leaving the bologna out on the kitchen counter after making a sandwich. That year, both my sister and her husband were instrumental in helping me transition from an irresponsible juvenile to an employed irresponsible juvenile.

Rosie helped me get my first job. It was a busboy gig at the New England Oyster House, a restaurant with a manager who took great pleasure in embarrassing her employees. Miss Peggy would run the restaurant like she was running a concentration camp. For example, she would insist that I clean and reset as many as ten tables in my section while simultaneously changing the sign on the marquee outside, at the speed of a rabbit jacked up on caffeine. One day, while putting up the daily special on the marquee, a strong wind knocked my ladder down, and I was stuck on the ledge more than 100 feet in the air. I immediately started calling for help and hoping someone would discover me before Miss Peggy noticed the dirty tables. When I was finally rescued about an hour later and reported to Miss Peggy the reason for my absence, she told me my being stranded was no excuse and then threatened to fire me the next time the wind left me on the ledge. I lasted only a few more weeks. The wind was really bad that winter.

As a kid, I always knew what I didn't want to be when I grew up. A grown-up. Adults were all so serious and boring. They seemed to have so many – responsibilities. The poor unfortunate souls. Ten to fourteen hours at work, then they fight traffic to come home to a cranky spouse and a house full of ungrateful kids. I would know. I was one of the ungrateful kids.

As a result of my tendency to fool around, I frustrated several employers. "I don't run a circus," I can still hear them saying. One such boss was quite fond of me. My brother and I worked for him as waiters in a very fancy restaurant. The kind that has a wine steward who brings you a wine menu, and if you don't mind paying a small fortune, he will bring you a bottle. Then you will sniff the cork like a dog before you swirl your glass around, looking at who knows what and if you think it's up to par, you drink some. This restaurant was so fancy that when our customers ordered a Caesar salad, we had Caesar come out and make it. Caesar was our waiter from Cuba, who was the best at making a salad from scratch.

One day, when there were hardly any customers in the restaurant, my brother and I started goofing around. Tommy worked with me in the restaurant, and that night, we worked at the same station. I thought it would be fun if I pretended to order a meal and Tommy pretended to be my waiter. I sat in a booth and asked Tommy for a menu.

"Here you are, sir," he said. "The special of the night is our Shrimp Scampi made fresh at the table with white wine lemon butter sauce and served over a bed of rice or linguini."

"That sounds quite splendid," I said with an English accent, "What is the catch of the day?" Tommy went on to explain the catch of the day and the other famous dishes our restaurant was known for. Then, my brother changed roles and sat at the table with me, pretending to be my dinner guest.

"So what looks good to you?" he says.

"Oh, my waiter just recommended the Shrimp Scampi," I responded. "What do you think?"

"I think I will try the…"

All of a sudden, our little skit was interrupted by a very tall, very stern-looking man standing at our table. It was Oscar, our boss, the restaurant's manager.

Ohhh shit, I thought to myself. Here were two waiters, sitting in a booth in a high-end restaurant, fully clothed in their formal waiter attire, complete with brown vest and tie, reading from the menu and looking like they were about to be jobless.

"Get your things," Oscar ordered, "and go home." I wanted to ask him if we should come back tomorrow but decided to let that be a surprise. Maybe if he had time to think about it, he would go from thinking he would fire us to just suspending us for a while, and we would be back in a couple of years.

Tommy and I went home, and we were almost in tears. Okay, we were in tears. Two grown men crying. We both loved our jobs. I felt really bad for Tommy. I helped him get this job only months earlier and now I had helped him get out of it. I got my little brother in trouble – again.

It seemed I had a habit of doing that. At home that night, Tommy and I collaborated on a letter of apology. We promised that we would never sit down at any booth ever again for the rest of our lives. Even now, when I go to a restaurant, I feel like I should find somewhere to sit that is not at a booth. Oscar accepted our letter of apology and reinstated us. You would think my days of fooling around on the job were over. They had only just begun.

The trouble I would get into was not unlike Jerry Lewis, Lucile Ball, or Bud Costello, except that their trouble was just pretend while mine was real. Few of the jobs I had as a young man appeared to suit me very well. When I was between high school and college, I had no idea what I should go to college to study. I was being told to pursue my passion which at the time was nothing. So, I pursued nothing.

That worked fine until I met a young lady who was not so impressed by my life-long pursuit of nothing. She seemed to prefer that I pursue something. She also seemed to think that I was highly talented and exceptionally capable. She clearly had no idea how committed I was to my pursuit of nothing, and unfortunately, I was successful for many years. Our first encounter should have been a clue to her to find someone else, but she tells me she saw something in me that she fell in love with. She has been trying to find that something ever since.

At eighteen years old, I had spent a whole year working odd jobs while trying to figure out my next step. It could well be that the jobs were quite normal, and it was me that was odd.

I knew I needed to go to college; I just didn't know what I would do once I got there.

Clowning around at college was clearly a popular student activity practiced by many students, but it did not result in any type of degree.

I eventually went to Bible College. I believe I ended up choosing to go to Bible College by default. It was de fault of my parents, who brought me up to believe in the Bible. I would also like to blame the clown who was the pastor of the church I attended at the time since he encouraged this decision, and his ministry was a real circus.

Being brought up in a Christian home, I had heard a lot of preaching by this point in my life, and much of it was sub-par. I believed I was pretty good at public speaking, having spoken to the young people at my local church and in several classrooms at school, and figured that my ability to speak and God's obvious need for good speakers meant that I would do a good job of preaching in church. So, the basic plan was to go to Bible College and become a pastor who would have a built-in audience to speak to every week. As it turns out, pastors do very little speaking and lots of other things like visiting sick people, asking for money (fundraising), listening to people's problems, building structures, conducting marathon staff meetings, and shaking lots of hands while saying God bless you to lots of people, some of whom I wouldn't like very much. I am not good at any of those things, especially listening to people's problems. I can barely deal with my problems. I don't need to hear yours.

But I am not entirely sorry that I spent four years studying the Bible. Especially when you consider how little I was actually studying. I am certainly not blaming the college for my lack of scholarship. I aimed at being a mediocre student, and I succeeded.

Plus, Bible College did a lot of good for me, starting with keeping me out of trouble. I courted my wife there, and after almost forty years of marriage, I can honestly say that I don't blame the college for the suffering this caused. When I look back at the years I was being groomed for church work, I see the direct and indirect connection it all had in preparing me for my eventual work in comedy. For starters, at Bible College, I learned how to handle rejection, a very important characteristic for professional funny people.

It was at the beginning of my second semester, and I was placed as the fifth student in a room with four basketball jocks. When they realized that I was assigned to room with them, they immediately had a dilemma. Basketball jocks don't hang with commoners. It's stated in a formal manual somewhere. The group chose the leading jock to tell me I needed to find another room. This is a Bible school, mind you, so he did it in a Christ-like way. He put his arm around me and asked very politely if there was any way possible for me to find another room. When I told him no, he pointed out that he and his roommates could make life hell for me. I did understand 'hell.' That was covered in the first semester. Needless to say, I found another room.

You could say God wanted me to go to Bible College as a stepping stone toward the next stop on my vocational train – 'Clowning.'

Jester In The Courtship

And then the lover,
Sighing like furnace, with woeful ballad
Made to his mistress' eyebrow.
William Shakespeare's As You Like It

Here is my take on this

And then the lover,
Singing romantic songs
About his lady's eyebrows
Ronnie Carrington's She Didn't Like It

I sat on an unflushable toilet filled with human waste and started adding my own crap to the sewer soup. Taking a dump in a commode that sat in plain view of several prison employees is no small feat. I had desperately tried to keep my shit together, having waited for more than three hours for someone to come and bail me out of the jail cell that two police officers had placed me in. Sure, I was driving with a suspended license, and yes, I did have an expired plate on my vehicle when they pulled me over. But this certainly did not justify getting handcuffed, placed in the back of their squad car and taken to Cutler Ridge Jail. Granted, it was more of a holding cell, but when I saw the bars and realized I would be on the opposite side of freedom, the difference was inconsequential.

Who knew such trivial oversight could be treated so harshly? I was driving my older brother Richard home and was within a block of his house when I was pulled over. When they asked me for my driver's license, I explained that I was a Bible college student on summer break and that I must have misplaced my wallet. This did

"

not improve their disposition toward me. Then, they asked me a series of questions that led them to discover I had left out some crucial information. My license had been suspended due to non-payment of a previous ticket. It was a lie of omission. Lying to the police, I now realize, was not a good idea, especially since I didn't get away with it. As I sat in the state trooper's vehicle, I noticed how slowly people drove by and how interested they were in my dilemma. I guess they were concerned for my well-being. Fortunately, they placed me in a cell by myself. I was in no mood to make new friends.

It was hard enough having to take a dump in a backed-up commode while sitting in the middle of a room open to the police staff. I have always had trouble taking a crap in public toilets. Maybe it's just me, but my taking a dump usually comes with lots of noises and smells I would rather not have other people subjected to. But between the flood of diarrhea that was pushing on the walls of my bowels and the stress created by being incarcerated, it was either the toilet or my pants. And I had other problems. That same afternoon, I had arranged to meet a young lady at an amusement park for a date and I was reasonably sure she would show up while I on the other hand would likely be a no show.

My date was not the kind of girl who would go out with men of questionable character. She certainly would not want to get involved with someone who broke the law and, even worse, ended up in jail. I knew this would not be a good first impression and, more than likely, I would not get a second chance to make any further impressions.

In any case, this was going to take some explaining on my part, and as I waited in that nasty, smelly jail cell, I certainly had the time to come up with some type of justification for my absence. I practiced my little speech.

"Sorry, I did not make it to our date. I was a bit held up due to being arrested, handcuffed, placed in the back of a squad car, and imprisoned. Want to reschedule for next Saturday at 6:00 p.m.?"

At 6:55 p.m., Richard came running into the police precinct with the $500 bond money needed to get me out of lockup. I remember the time because the jailer called me a lucky man, considering my brother had arrived 5 minutes before all prisoners were to be transported to the downtown jail to spend the night. In the downtown jail, you had no choice but to make friends with other incarcerated men, and I'm really a very shy person.

A few months later, I found out that the date I stood up was planning on enrolling in the same college I had been attending. This, I figured, would give me more opportunities to impress this young lady. Now, all I had to do was make sure to renew my automobile tag, pay my previously unpaid tickets, get my driver's license reinstated, and start living like a responsible adult. No problem. Now, I had a woman I was very interested in courting, and I had to get my act together. It was time to get serious about life.

Back at Bible College, I was showing my new lady friend around the campus and helping her get acclimated with her new school. I had been dating a few girls at the time and wanted to keep those options open, so I kept reminding my new friend that we were not dating and that she was free to go out with any guy she liked. Her first date request came only a few weeks later from a guy named Timmy, whom, upon meeting, I immediately disliked. He was quite a gentleman, good-looking, very smart, and quite charming, which was precisely why I didn't like him. Her first date with Timmy went wonderfully, and she had a great time. Damn it. She told me how he brought her flowers and chocolate, and he opened the door for her and pulled out her seat in the fine restaurant they dined at! Then she described how he was so charming, sensitive, and thoughtful and that she thought she might go out with him again. Holy crap! Now it was clear if I didn't move fast, I was going to lose my girl to this Timmy dude.

When she came back from the second date, I questioned her.

"Where did you go"? I asked.

"Out to dinner," she replied, only giving up what she felt was necessary. "Did he try to kiss you?" I inquired.

"I thought you said you didn't mind if I went out with other men?" she asked.

"Well, ahhh, yeah, see, I don't mind you going out; I just want to know how it went?"

"It went great," she said.

All I could think about the next few hours was whether this Timmy character was snuggling, cuddling, smooching, and otherwise stealing away my girlfriend. The no-good, rotten scumbag. The next day, after a sleepless night, I asked her if she wanted to go on a date with me.. A real date.[13] I told her my plans, what time I would pick her up, and how I would make the reservations. She said I would have to wait for her answer; she would have to pray about it. Pray about it? What was there to pray about? We had been friends for weeks, and she knew I was a really nice guy, right? Well, except for being in jail, talking a lot, not being a gentleman, and being broke. Every day over the next week, I checked with my lady friend if she had gotten an answer from God, and every day, she told me she hadn't heard back from Him yet. How long did

---

[13] The kind of date where I paid for her dinner, pulled out her chair, and did other gentlemanly-type stuff too.

God take to answer a prayer for direction on going out with a nice guy? Finally, God had given her the peace and direction she needed, and she told me she would accept my formal dinner date.

As we spent time together at college, I noticed my new lady friend really appreciated my sense of humor, and I appreciated her appreciation of my sense of humor. Eventually, she became my biggest fan, and I worked on entertaining her as much as possible.

Like the time we left the college library where we had been whispering instead of studying. As we walked outside, I noticed that we continued to speak in a very soft voice, and I said to her, in a whisper, "Why are we still whispering?" She laughed so loud people back in the library could hear us. When I goofed around, she seemed to find me quite amusing, and this was very important to me since I was broke at the time, and goofing around was all the entertainment I could afford. I thought she was quite interesting too, and the first day I kissed her, things went from interesting to hot and heavy. Over time, we became best friends, and I was glad to have a friend with whom I could fool around.

One day, I was driving my new girlfriend home from a dinner date, and I made a mistake and ended up on a bridge going toward a town in the opposite direction of our college. It was a very long bridge, so I knew we would be going the wrong way for quite some time and I was embarrassed.

"Don't worry," she said. "As long as I'm with you, I am happy," and in that moment, I knew she was my type of woman[14] and wanted to marry her. Then we filled the extra 60 minutes of driving time happily chatting and laughing.

I never understood why society promoted strange and unnatural

---

[14] The type who could deal with my goof-ups.

traditions as signs that a man was a proper suitor. Why on earth should I walk all the way around the car to open the door on the lady's side so she could get out? Was she too weak to pull on the door handle herself? How was this in any way, an indication that I cared about her? I saw this as a perfect waste of time and often said so. But this young lady seemed quite unimpressed by my lack of etiquette and was determined to do something about it. One day, I got out of the car and walked to the front door of the school cafeteria, and I noticed that she was still sitting in the car. After walking the 150 feet or so back to the car to open her door, I spent the rest of the evening with a woman who had a troubled look on her face. A look that said, "I'm not sure this relationship is going to work out." I remember thinking the same thing. Over time, her list of poor behaviors that needed fixing continued to grow. Prominent on the list was that I placed large amounts of food in my mouth all at once. One day, she added that I should not talk while the food was still being chewed. Really? Why not? Why do I have to change my preferred eating habits because one woman didn't like it? What's next, I have to stop scratching my ass in front of people? What if we got married, and she found out I liked to piss in the sink? Or fart in public? What was she going to think when she saw me pick my nose? In church? Just before preaching?

I was worried about my woman's apparent lack of tolerance for my lack of decorum and having now been married to the woman for close to 40 years, I can tell you I was on to something.

I remember how in order to make the point that seeing chewed food was only a perceived lack of civility, I would place food in my mouth and open it as wide as possible, thereby exposing all the contents therein to my girlfriend and try to nudge a laugh out of her very disapproving face. She never did find that so damn funny. In fact, I recall her expression communicating a desire to see me choke. Which, on at least one occasion, I did. And she responded that it served me right.

Clothing choices were also an area that she felt obligated to provide her unsolicited expertise. Every day, I wore the same old jeans with the tattered, frayed bottom, and every time she saw me in them, she cringed as if she had just seen a dead rat. I had a sort of a relationship with those jeans. We went back way further than my new girlfriend, having faithfully covered the lower part of my body since my days in junior college. In addition, these pants were the only piece of clothing that did not require the strange human habit called 'washing' since they hardly showed any dirt. They didn't need ironing either. The caked-on dirt worked as a sort of starch, and those pants could stand up entirely on their own. But the new woman in my life felt it was her duty to lobby for the permanent banishment of these perfectly innocent pants. She wanted them thrown out and replaced by jeans that were new. Unbelievable!

The request for my permanent separation from the items I owned for years did not stop with my clothing. My old tennis bag with the torn zipper – get rid of it. My nap sack book bag – sorry, it's not up to par. Even my only form of transportation, a 10-year-old Chevy Monza that would start most of the time, was being targeted for replacement. This new girlfriend was going to cost me some cold, hard cash.

Dating this woman was getting to be tricky. She apparently had big plans for me, and they all involved me changing in some way, shape, or form, and some of these shapes I didn't think I could form. She seemed to see me as a 'fixer-upper' that needed a lot of work. There were problems with my plumbing; lots of walls had to come down, my paint was peeling, my wires were crossed, the beams were unsecure, there were holes in my roof, and I think she considered my whole foundation unstable. But I had potential. Probably because she liked my layout.

Eventually, breaking up with my new girlfriend became a common occurrence. One week, we were seen sitting beside each other in class, holding hands under the desk; the next week, we were sitting at least two rows apart, exchanging occasional glances and trying with all our might to stay detached. One day, we were definitely not talking to each other, and the following day, we were getting married. Such was the personality of our relationship. On or off, hot or cold, break up or get married; this was one wild roller coaster ride of courtship, and it was both fun and scary as hell. Two people, trying to decide if saying "I do" at an altar was truly the right thing to do or saying "I'm done" was indeed the more prudent option. Would it last? Was it safe to commit my whole life to this person? Was she going to make me happy or drive me crazy? Was she going to comfort me or annoy me? Was she going to be a blessing or a curse? As it turns out – a mixture of all of the above.

Whatever was going to happen, this was going to be some adventure. Sit back, buckle yourself in, keep your feet and elbows inside the ride at all times, hold on to the bar in front of you, and whatever you do, do not attempt to exit until the ride has come to a complete stop. Oh my god, where is this ride taking me? Why are we going so high? This looks very dangerous, oh ohhhhh – wheeeeee!

Every day we spent together further cemented our relationship, and I knew the night I said those three powerful words I was not going anywhere anytime soon.

During our first semester together, we decided to attend the College Bar B Que known as Sadie Hawkins, a traditional event where the woman asks the man to go instead of the other way around. It was not surprising that she asked me to go as I had asked her to do so. Later that night, I allowed the three words that every man gets tempted to say to the girl he likes very much to slip out of my mouth and into her ears. "I love you," I told her, and she responded, "I love you too."

Then we kissed under a moonlit sky with so much passion I reconsidered my Christian pledge to celibacy. Chemicals in her brain registered my statement as a commitment to love and to cherish her till death do you part. She started to think about where she wanted to go on her honeymoon, where she wanted us to live, and what job she wanted me to have. I do not understand the phenomenon. All I know is that the look in her eyes from that moment on was – 'you are mine and mine alone.' It was like being at an auction and accidentally bidding the highest bid on something you were not sure you wanted and hearing the words, "Sold – to the gentleman with the stunned look for more than he was prepared to pay." What? Who? Me? Why? What the #%@#?

What had become clear to me was that this very attractive young lady was, without a doubt, my very best friend. Life was so much more fulfilling, so much more meaningful with her in it. Our conversations were like a ballet of words, deeply rewarding and completely engaging. Sharing was effortless and sincere, and there was a clear absence of pretense. I had never realized that conversation could be so much fun, and it had not dawned on me how essential this connection of the mind was to a long-term relationship. Not every man falls in love with someone they also like. I was not going to let her get away.

Eventually, I got the part, and she married me. She was to become my leading lady and the greatest addition to my show. What is even more important is that my wife still cuts me some slack when I screw things up, and I still make her laugh when we are going over the wrong bridge. She clearly had no idea how often I would be lost. But she seems to enjoy every minute of it. Minus a few in which I was being a complete jerk.

Games People Play

Then a soldier,
Full of strange oaths,
and bearded like the pard,
Jealous in honour,
sudden and quick in quarrel,
Seeking the bubble reputation
Even in the cannon's mouth.
William Shakespeare's As You Like It

Here is my take on this

Then a guy trained to fight
Full of youthful conviction
Jealous and ready to argue
Even when facing death
Ronnie Carrington's Nobody Likes It

In December 1985, I had only been married a few months, but I could already tell my wife was taking this marriage thing very seriously. In fact, unlike me, who took very little seriously, she took on every task with the focus of an Olympic gymnast performing in front of grumpy Romanian judges. It didn't matter if she was working on a college degree or playing a friendly game of checkers. She was completely driven to win, and I made the mistake once of competing against her in Scrabble, only to realize we would have to contact the inventor of the game to clarify some of the rules she was determined I would follow. I have never seen her do anything half-hearted or even three-quarter-hearted, and I have long given up challenging her at anything since I really hate getting my ass beat.

Chess, billiards, Chinese checkers, Scrabble, Monopoly, hopscotch, bumper cars, truth or dare are all out of the question.

One of the only A's I received in college was directly related to the fact that I took the course with my then 'wife-to-be.' She sat beside me in class, doing strange things like taking notes and listening to the teacher. Then, when we were to have a test the next day, she would call me to see how far I had gotten in my studies.

"What do you think Professor Richardson meant when he told us to evaluate the history of the church in relationship to the Calvinistic doctrine of predestination and the Lutheran doctrine of sanctification through grace?" she might ask. "We have a test on this tomorrow."

"We have a test tomorrow?" I remember asking.

"Yes, it's on the syllabus."

You read that stuff? I recall wondering.

After she explained everything to me and went over her notes, I was reasonably prepared for the test. Add to the equation the pressure I felt knowing she would want to know my grade, and this would force me to study all night long. This scenario was repeated enough times that I eventually received an A in Professor Richardson's class. Unfortunately, my girlfriend did not take any of the other classes required to complete my degree, and my test scores suffered terribly.

After we got married, we were in Jamaica on vacation, and the hotel we were staying at hosted a big Bar-B-Que-Bash, complete with a live Reggae band, volleyball, fashion show and special game. The winner of the game would receive a free scuba diving adventure for two, worth more than $500. Six couples were chosen to play amongst the hundreds in attendance. My wife and I were chosen. What happened next is both hilarious and disturbing at the same time.

They blindfolded the ladies, arranged the husbands in a straight line, and unbeknownst to the six women who were blindfolded, added 15 additional men to the line. Then they explained to the blindfolded women that they were to try to find their husbands only by touch. Absolutely no talking; not even a grunt would be allowed. When the wife thought she found her husband she was to kiss him on the lips. And if she got to the end of the line and did not find her husband, she had 60 seconds to run back and find him. Kiss the right man, and you win. Kiss the wrong man, and you would have one happy man.

They brought out the first contestant. She nervously touched the first man's face, and only for a split second. It looked like she was putting her hand in a bowl of raw eggs. In fact, she barely touched any of the men, and she never did find her husband. The next woman they brought out repeated a similar set of mild touches. She also failed.

By the time they got to my wife, not one woman had found her husband. They placed my bride at the top of the line in front of the first man. She grabbed the stranger by the head and ran her hands firmly down the contours of his completely surprised face like she was sculpting a statue out of clay. She did not miss a single detail, taking in and calculating every feature, dimple, and hair follicle. That first man got such a thorough checking out, from head to toe, I believe he actually enjoyed it.

Then my wife repeated this very slow, very deliberate search with her hands on each man in the line. It dawned on me at one point when she was checking out a man twice my size, with muscles coming out from places where I would have fat instead, that she might be having a good time herself.

Finally, my wife was standing directly in front of me. The judges were watching very closely to make sure we did not cheat in any way. They had exchanged my T-shirt for a sleeveless marina and placed a hat on my head to throw her off. My wife was very meticulous. She started at the top, and upon coming across the hat, threw it to the ground, running her hands through my hair and all around my scalp. Then she graduated to my face, pressing against my eyebrows and forehead before moving to my nose and lips. Finally, it seemed she was sure it was me. Maybe it was the face, maybe it was my extra-large tummy, but she stood there, unmoving and confident she had finally found her man and gave me a big kiss on the lips.

Then they did something that was unexpected. Before taking off my wife's blindfold, they pulled me out of the line and inserted another man with the same build and similar feature set to me. As they took her blindfold off, she looked up and saw him instead of me and thought she had just kissed the wrong man. I was now standing in a crowd of people trying desperately to explain the situation. I will never forget my wife's look at that moment. She was horrified that she had failed to kiss me and had, in fact, passionately kissed another man. The game organizers were trying to keep me from telling her the truth to juice this joke as long as possible. They were holding me back and the crowd was cheering so loud my wife could not hear me. The man she thought she had kissed was playing it up and dancing around like he just had the time of his life. My wife's eyes began to fill with tears. "I'm sorry," she mouthed. I tried to mouth words back to her. It was hard to come up with two or three words that would clarify everything. How was I to mouth – "It's okay because you did kiss me, but they took me out of the line and replaced me with that guy just before they took off your blindfold?"

A minute later, they let me run over to her and tell her the truth.
Now we were hugging, crying, laughing and relieved all at once

Wanna Party?

And then the justice,
In fair round belly with good capon lin'd,
With eyes severe and beard of formal cut,
Full of wise saws and modern instances;
And so he plays his part.
William Shakespeare's As You Like It

Here is my take on this

And then the justice,
When you are fat and sporting a beard,
And full of yourself,
You keep acting
Ronnie Carrington's Only You Like It

Years after getting married it became clear that 'entertainer' was a viable vocation. I had been clowning around since I was old enough to drool and it came naturally for me to do so in front of an audience. My wife and I worked on a business name that would double as our individual stage names.

Cookies and Cream, Peanut Butter and Jelly, and Macaroni and Cheese were all considered but did not make the final cut. Then it hit us. My wife claims it hit her first but, in my mind, it bounced off of me and then it hit her. Either way, we had found our clown names. 'Sugar and Spice.' Of course, she, being the sweet person that she is, was to be Sugar. And I, being well 'Hot,' would be Spice. Shortly thereafter she began her insistence that we practice before we perform. I had the same response I had to her insistence that we study when we were in college. Let's practice later. This generally meant, on the way to the event. I would soon find out my wife was allergic to last-minute preparation.

During the first clown skit my wife and I ever performed together, I almost killed her. By accident of course. The skit required that I throw a bucket of confetti in her face. Easy enough. Except that I threw the confetti at the precise moment she opened her mouth and things did not go well from there. She was supposed to act annoyed with me (which should have come easily) and then chase me with a plastic baseball bat, but she was too busy choking (due to the confetti that was stuck in her throat). In fact, she was on the floor gasping for air and the audience didn't know whether to laugh or call 911. I made a few jokes about the hacking sounds she was making and then we stopped the performance so I could whack her in the back, and she could spit up wads of colored paper. I guess we should have practiced. She survived, but we retired that routine, and years later, the character. Sugar and Spice would need to decide that their marriage was more important than their clown act. And both acts could not survive concurrently. Thus, I became a one man show.

The things that can go wrong when performing are diverse. On one occasion the poodle that does tricks for the big finale in my show came out on stage and immediately the kids started laughing. I assumed that I was doing something funny and felt good about it until I looked around and saw my dog pooping in the middle of the stage. And he took his time too. At least he tried to cover the poop by using his hind legs to cover it with dirt. That show went to crap.

On another occasion, my wife and I had a disagreement just before the show started. She felt that I had spoken to her inappropriately and I felt that it was quite appropriate. Her response to this was to let me introduce her and then not appear with me on stage. There I was standing in front of hundreds of kids with my leading lady nowhere in sight. I kept saying, "Ladies and gentlemen, give a big round of applause for Sugar the clown and then pointing to the spot she was supposed to appear. But there was no Sugar. By now I was thinking some very bad things about Sugar the clown, including having her replaced. She did eventually appear but not until she made sure I knew not to insult her just before the show began. I did learn my lesson. From that day on I waited till after the show to insult her.

After you have things go badly in front of a live audience you start doing the one thing an entertainer should never do. You start to sweat. People know when you, the performer, are nervous and they begin to feel nervous for you. Not the emotion you want them to have during a show. Basically, rule number one for any type of entertainer is to pretend that you are having a good time. Trust me, when you see the performers having a good time, they are just acting. Just beneath that smile is absolute terror.

Standing in front of a live audience is nerve-wracking, intimidating, and terribly frightening no matter how many times you have done it. At times I have had to do shows under the most hideous of conditions. I had to do the show in Sahara Desert-type heat. That was one hot show. In the space the size of a broom closet. That was a tight show. With dogs sniffing out my show bunnies. That show went to the dogs. With drunk fathers standing on the stage area. A horror show. And on one occasion with near hurricane-force winds. That show blew everyone away.

I have done shows in which the adults were standing around speaking so loudly that even with my sound system turned way up I could hardly be heard. That's usually when one of the adults asks me to turn down my sound system so they can talk. Sometimes I stop the show and address the wayward adults by saying, "I'm sorry is my show interrupting your conversation?" That doesn't always work. Some of the adults have threatened to do terrible things to me.

The distractions I have to deal with are sometimes so outrageous I feel like I am doing the show for myself. I may have twenty little hyper-active five-year-olds sitting in front of me looking for a reason to be distracted and here comes the mommy walking up and down in front of the stage, with hot dogs and sodas. Lady, I'm trying to do a show here. Can we feed them later? Then the photographer jumps in front of me to take what he thinks is the perfect picture of the birthday boy. All I need now is for the Sponge Bob character they hired to show up early and start waving at the kids. Damn, here comes Sponge Bob.

I did a birthday party once where the birthday boy walked up on my stage and started going through my magic tricks. When I told him he could not be on my stage he said ,"this is not your property." He was right. I was on his property. I later found out the kid's father was a lawyer.

At another show my four-year-old volunteer kicked me smack dab in my knee. The bad one. Well, it wasn't bad then, but it is now. When I smiled and told him not to do that, he kicked me in my other bad knee. I was visually upset and that really got him going, especially since the audience was laughing. He kept kicking my knees and then running from me while I tried to grab him. As this was happening, I announced, "Will the parent of the four-year-old who is on stage kicking me please come up to collect your child." No one moved. I scanned the audience for evidence of an undercover parent. The kid was now kicking my legs from behind. I decided to ignore him in favor of tracking down his parole officer.

It was then that I had the bright idea to yell out "Security!" and there was a roar of laughter from the audience. Unfortunately, no one moved. I was on my own. I grabbed the kid with both hands and looked him straight in the eyes and with the most serious face a man with a spinning propeller hat could muster I said, "Look kid, you can't keep kicking me like that." To which he stepped on my foot with all his might. More laughter from the crowd. The whole thing played out like a comedy routine except I was not laughing and would soon need medical assistance.

After the show, two adults came up to me to congratulate me on a very entertaining performance and to tell me that the four-year-old monster child who abused me was none other than their little Johnny. I wanted so badly to ask them why they had not saved me from my near-death experience, but I didn't want them to know that I was bothered by Johnny's violence in any way. Besides, I knew why they hadn't. They had no control over Johnny either. Johnny would have kicked their ass.

But most kids are very nice people. They live life without all the hang-ups and prejudices that adults often have. A three-year-old may tell me he doesn't like my hat but he is unlikely to tell me he doesn't like a particular race, religion, or political party. They haven't learned who to hate. We have to teach them that as time goes on.

One day I was at a private school doing a show for about forty little kids. In the classroom watching the show were their teacher and her assistant. A few minutes into the performance I started my comedy routine in which I told the kids I was not allowed to dance to the music because it was a serious magic show. Then my body starts moving to the music and I pretend I can't help it. The kids spontaneously erupt into laughter, a phenomenon that is fairly typical at this point in the presentation. Some of the kids laugh loudly showing their teeth, others giggle with their mouths wide open and some respond with what sounds like snickering. The senior teacher stops the show, quiets the kids, and says, "Now children, that is not how you respond to something funny. Let's show Spice the clown how well-behaved you can be. When you hear something funny you are supposed to say ha ha ha. Now let's do it together – ha ha ha"

I was in shock. The kids had been laughing at me hysterically but had been stopped so that the teacher could teach them how they were supposed to laugh. I ignored her and continued my silly antics which triggered more laughter. However, the teacher refused to let the kids make their own individual sounds of approval. There were too many variations for her liking. It was not organized enough for her. She continued to explain to these three and four-year-olds that the sound coming from their mouths must sound like this, "ha ha ha." And she was dead serious.

As I have grown older, I have tried very hard not to act like the big people. I refuse to be sucked into a world where we are confined by adult norms. I know I cannot avoid my eventual assimilation into the grown-up world, I am just trying to postpone it. I do not want to let go of the world of wonder I had when I was six, the innocence of believing that family would support me unconditionally, or the excitement I felt when it was time to play.

Cutting It Close

I arrived at the party to perform my clown magic show with justifiable anxiety. I was after all, new to performing and especially nervous about wealthy clients. The event was in a well-to-do Miami neighborhood, and I noticed that almost every other car was a Mercedes Benz, BMW or similar fancy car I will never own. Trying to park my old SUV hooked to my eight-foot rusty trailer so that I did not scratch anyone's car was tricky, even for a magician. When I knocked on the huge mahogany door the father of the birthday girl, a large Italian man, welcomed my wife and me in and introduced us to his family. There was his mother, his grandmother, his cousin Luey, his thirty-something-year-old nephew, Vinnie and the four-year-old birthday girl, Gabrielle.

Vinnie was a stocky guy who deliberately wore extra-short shirt sleeves in order to reveal his quite impressive biceps. When I offered to shake his hand, he glared at me as if offended and squeezed my hand like he was trying to extract juice from a grapefruit.

"Don't I know yuz from somewhere?" he inquired. His demeanor suggested he was agitated by my existence. I don't think he liked clowns.

"No, I don't think so," I assured him. "We've never met."

"I know you, your name is Johnny," he says while standing so close I could smell the gum he was chewing. Double mint.

"No," I repeated.

Vinnie shook his head. Then he walked away seemingly unconvinced. I was left wondering if this guy was serious or just messing with me. I started my set up in the living room where I had been directed. It was a spacious area decorated with plush curtains, exotic lamps, several statues, large paintings and ornaments that I knew I had better not break. One lady warned me to be careful when I got too close to a statue telling me where it came from and how irreplaceable it was. Vinnie kept his eyes on me as if he thought I may pocket one of the ornaments. He gave me the creeps. Perhaps I had watched too many gangster movies, I told myself.

Finally, it was time for the show to start and I decided to open with one of my newest magic tricks ... the hand cutter. This trick was really impressive. Unfortunately, the first time I tried it I nicked the volunteer's arm and drew blood. Nobody's perfect.

The hand cutter was a menacing device that looked like a cross between a large kitchen utensil and a small guillotine. It had been sold to me by a clown who also had trouble with injuring his volunteers. I should have realized then that this trick was for real magicians.

You know, the kind who actually practice their craft. My practice took place during the live event. I needed the extra adrenalin to ward off boredom. The secret to this prop was to time the blades descent toward the arm, pulling it back with a small lever at the last minute so it barely missed cutting into flesh. I was clearly not ready for the level of expertise this prop required but on this day, I had no other option. The crowd of mostly middle-aged Italian men, two notches past tipsy, one notch short of clown abuse, seemed eager to fire off unfavorable opinions and I didn't want to give them ammunition. A corny magic trick wouldn't do. The show started and I asked for a volunteer who would place their hand in the chopper. None of the kids seemed eager to volunteer. These were smart kids. But Mr.

Corleone himself volunteered Vinnie.

"Hey, Vinnie, get up there and help Spice with his magic trick" the man of the house insisted.

I had wanted a five-year-old boy to come up. If I had accidently cut his hand I could have simply given him a band aid, a signed picture, an honest apology, and been on my way. Vinnie, on the other hand, seemed apt to place my nuts in a coffee grinder, my body still attached. But Vinnie was opposed to coming up on stage. He seemed genuinely worried about the hand cutter trick going wrong.

"Nah, it's okay," he said. "Why not let one of the kids have the honor?"
"Yeah, how about we use a kid," I chimed in.

But the Godfather would not relent.

"Vinnie get up on stage and help Spice," he insisted. Vinnie had no choice. He strode up on stage. The family cheered as he stood beside me, looking at the contraption and its large blade, and then looking at me.

The routine with the hand chopper called for pretending I was unsure of myself. I didn't have to pretend.

"Ladies and gentlemen," I announced. "I will now attempt to place Vinnie's hand inside the chopper and bring the blade down through his hand … without injury… hopefully." People snickered and Vinnie gave me a serious look.

"Do you have insurance, Vinnie?" I asked as a joke. He didn't seem to think it was funny.

"If anything bad happens, you're the one that's gonna need insurance," Vinnie responded." I felt sick. At the time I didn't have insurance.

"You sure you know what you're doing?" Vinnie asked.

I placed Vinnie's arm inside the device, just below the blade. The audience was completely engaged. They knew that if I screwed this up Vinnie would have no problem exacting revenge. I tried to look calm but the sweat that had formed on my face revealed my fear.

"Hey Vinnie, don't worry, I rarely screw this up," I tell him. "But just in case, is there a doctor in the house?"

Vinnie was now sweating along with me.

"Abra Hocus Comocus Yabadabadoo Iminabigtrouble … what's that magic word again?" I asked.

The kids yelled out, "Abracadabra!"

Suddenly, I brought the handle down and watched as the blade passed within millimeters of Vinnie's arm while appearing to pass through. The room erupted in applause and laughter. The audience was genuinely impressed with my apparent expertise. Vinnie was visibly relieved. He seemed sincerely grateful that I spared him the trouble of having to break my legs, and I was even more thankful to have saved him the extra work.

After the show, when I was packing up and getting ready to leave, the Big Kahuna came over to me. "Great show" he said. "I love how you had Vinnie squirming."

"Thanks, it was fun," I lied, making sure to keep a straight face.

Funny Bunny

Many years ago, I got into a hobby that I admit is not typical of men my age. Or men of any age for that matter. I discovered a rabbit breeder in Homestead, Florida who had several breeds that were absolutely irresistible. I bought one to use in my magic show. But then I thought the girl bunny looked so lonely in her cage. So I got her a bunny friend. I should have gotten her a girl bunny friend but I didn't. Ooops.

Eventually, the bunny farm I bought the rabbits from started carrying several breeds. Lion heads, Floppy-eared, Rex, Dutch and Dwarf. I got two of each.

I often perform a routine in which I tell my audience that I will bring out my bag of stuffed bunnies so I can juggle them. After I place three or four fake bunnies on the table, I reach in to get the last one. But this last one is real. I place the real bunny on the table beside the assortment of stuffed ones. And the kids go wild shouting, "It's real." I explain that some bunnies look real but are not. When they tell me the rabbit is moving, I tell them some of the stuffed bunnies have batteries and that's why they can move. Then I tell the kids I will pick them all up and juggle them. Pandemonium ensues with kids desperately trying to tell me that one of the bunnies is alive, but I ignore them. It is not until I am about to throw the real bunny in the air that I do a double take and discover that indeed there is a real bunny mixed in with the stuffed ones.

The routine is a perfect way to get kids involved and a great way to introduce one of my bunnies. One day I decided to do the same routine but use two real bunnies instead of one. I figured I could get double the excitement with two. I went through my routine and held up each bunny before placing them on the table. Just as I expected the kids were shouting out that there were two live bunnies on the table behind me. In order to juice the joke, I made sure not to look at the bunnies. As the kids shouted louder and louder I started to notice a few phrases of particular interest.

"They're fighting. He's on top of her. They're doing it," were some of the remarks that stirred my curiosity. When I finally looked around, I saw what all the commotion was about. I had placed a male and a female bunny on the table and they were, how shall I say this delicately – getting their groove on. He was mowing her lawn. Doing the cha cha, makin' whoopie, hiding his pickle. In front of thirty kids. I had some splainin' to do. But while I was trying to convince the children that the bunnies were just grooming each other, a 6-year-old kid shouted out, "They're having sex!"

I Need Help

I really do love being a clown. I don't advertise this, but I love making people laugh so much, I often do it for free. For example, every day I try to make my wife laugh. No charge.

I know I should seek help so that eventually I can get a real job. One that provides a steady income, job security, and benefits. But apparently, I am doomed to a life of frivolity unless someone sets up an intervention.

I figure I am going to come home one day from a birthday party show to find my whole family sitting around my living room, imploring me to admit my addiction to clowning around and urging me to get on a bus that will take me to 'clown rehab.' Some, with real concern, will say, "Ron, we love you and don't want to see you waste your life with all this frivolity. You need serious help. Who knows, you may end up on the streets clowning for strangers, or even worse, you might be tempted to join the circus. Then, you will end up with no house or mortgage to pay, no leased car to drive, no cable TV to watch, no lawn to cut, no boss to answer to and wildly carefree. We want to save you from that life of hell and help you get a real job, at a bank, or retail store, where you can work yourself up to assistant manager. Listen to us. You cannot clown around your entire life. Now, stop making those faces, take off the silly hat, put down the oversized rubber chicken, return the bunny rabbit to his cage, and get on the bus with all the other loony clowns so we can take you to the funny farm where you can get help."

At clown rehab, I can imagine group therapy. "Hello, my name is Ronnie, and I am a clown addict. It's been two days since my last joke, and I am dying to make somebody laugh. Did you know that kids pick their noses and think it's candy, but it's snot. Do you like my shoes? They're made out of banana skins. They call them slippers. You buy them by the bunch, not by the pair. They appeal to me." Somebody in the group snickers and the staff hauls them off to electric shock therapy. "I lost my job because of sickness," I continue. "The boss got sick of me." One of the group therapists tells me to stop honking the bike horn at the end of every sentence. I continue upset that they have taken away my prop, I start speaking like Donald Duck. Now the doctors really think I'm a quack.

I know that when I have stress, I should deal with it like everybody else and just take the medications they give me. Those medications have been created by people who really care about my well-being. Taking them will help me be completely unfunny, like serious people. And they tell me I will have no more trouble. Except maybe very mild side effects like headaches, sleeplessness, depression, sudden heart failure, and possible death.

Over the years, I have been told to quit clowning around. Except when I am hired to do so. But I have never quite been able to deal with the disrespect I have to endure from so many who think my clown job is a joke.

Like the time I arrived at an elementary school in my clown outfit, and the custodian took one look at me and said, "Well, I guess you gotta do what you gotta do." At the time, I thought of several things I wanted to say to this gentleman, but I was concerned that a kid might hear me, and I would forever tarnish their image of clowns. "Hey, Mommy, the clown at school today told the custodian to take his toilet plunger and stick it up his…"

Sometimes I picture myself laying on a big leather couch, across from a bearded elderly gentleman in a white lab coat, holding a large chart, looking down at me over his glasses, with a serious expression of concern combined with a clear aura of superiority. I am the one after all that is lying on the 'need-serious-help-couch.' In my daydream, I would be saying "Help me Doc, I can't go on anymore. People don't respect clowns, they mistreat us, and often fail to acknowledge us," to which he would say "Next clown please."

I tell him how terrible I feel when people call me names and belittle my vocation and he says, "Look you, moron, you need to get a life, a real job and stop whining." Before I leave, I would explain that I have multiple personalities and he would charge me three times.

Sometimes my daydream has a psychiatrist trying to figure out why I would be so senseless as to choose to be a professional clown and why I was so preoccupied with humor.

"What comes to your mind when I say circus?" he might ask. "Clown," I would respond.

"Okay, what if I say, performer?" … "Clown."

"Funny?" … "Clown."

"Happy?" … "Clown."

"Sad?" … "Clown."

"Bad driver?" … "Damn clown."

"School teacher?" … "Boring clown."

"Charlie Chaplin?" … "Famous clown."

"Local congressman?" … "Lying clown."

"Rocket scientist?" … "Smart clown."

"Bozo?" … "Some guy."

Then he would check my answers and tell me I have a rare incurable disease known as 'Giggleitist.' This serious disease he will explain infects the heart with excessive merriment and leads to possible side-splitting hilarity. Those infected will notice a rise in highly toxic levels of hysterical chuckling, convulsive snickering, and even fatal hyperventilating. Eventually, the disease will spread throughout the body with chronic levels of amusement, leaving the sufferer in stitches, unable to sit up straight and be serious. Symptoms include rolling on the floor, gasping for air, holding one's belly, teary eyes, and strange loud cackling sounds emanating from the throat and mouth. Finally, the body will crack up and the inflicted will die laughing. One can catch this deadly disease by coming into close contact with funny people, professional comedians, amusing situations, or family members who know how to tickle your funny bone. If you are very young (under 18 months) the individual may contract the sickness when the carrier blows into the child's belly button, thereby creating vulgar farting-type sounds. In the worst cases, when the afflicted seems way too happy,[15] the patient may need a funny bone marrow transplant.

Possible treatments include long exposure to people with no sense of humor, reading and listening to hours of depressing news, driving in Miami rush hour traffic, or talking politics and religion with narrow-minded bigots. That should wipe the smile right off your face.

Frankly, I am hoping to infect as many people as possible with this disease, knowing that with comedy, if my timing is on and I

---

[15] My wife has regular bouts of extreme happiness. I recommended watching the news but she refused and went instead to the beach with our dogs, where she was seen frolicking in the sand. The poor woman. She insists on staying plagued with excessive merriment.

deliver enough 'punch' lines, I will 'knock 'em dead.' The result will be one 'killer act,' and everybody in my audience will be riddled with the 'giggles.

One Of My Favorite Acts

When I was a child, I would be the one who would not be satisfied with just adding tuna and mayo to bread when making a tuna sandwich. I ended up mixing in chopped onions, green peppers, mustard, crushed hard-boiled eggs, ketchup, sugar, sliced apple and my secret sauce. I would then melt cheese on the buttered bread making what I called a melted cheese and tuna salad supreme on a toasted sesame bun. Often, we would not have very many ingredients and I would have to make something called a formula. It was as if I was a chemist in a lab making a new compound out of a unique combination of elements. One of my formulas consisted of condensed milk, cocoa, sugar, vanilla, nutmeg, cinnamon, water, crushed ice, and should my mom have been in one of her more carefree-spending moods – ice cream. My concoctions would eventually gain a reputation for being exotic, and I was often asked by family members to make a formula for them.

Early in my marriage, my wife adopted the role of cooking and I, the role of handyman. My wife was not a bad cook. The problem arose because of what I came to see as extreme fussiness and detail. When cooking something she would do ridiculous things like measure to get the right amount.

Often, she would yell out to me…

"Was it one spoon of sugar in that tuna sandwich, Sweetheart, or two?" "Just put a pinch," I would respond. I had never measured anything in my life.

"Do you peel the apples before you chop them up or do you chop them with the peel?"

"Either way, Babe," I would say, "Throw caution to the wind."

"What type of mustard do you use? Honey mustard, hot mustard, or Grey Poupon?"

After about the fifth or sixth question, I would put down my newspaper, get up from the couch, and proceed to make the sandwich myself while she would take my place on the couch and pick up my newspaper. I could swear I heard her smiling behind the newspaper while I created my tuna sandwich masterpiece. When the meal she was cooking was actually complicated the questions were endless and I would always end up taking over and thinking how genius a plan my wife had devised. Pretend not to know how to prepare the meal and eventually, my husband will prepare it for me. I fell for it every time.

In truth, I was better suited to taking care of the food, especially when it involved multiple guests. Everything my wife does is methodical and although this is great when writing a doctoral dissertation, this does not always play out well when making ten different dishes for twenty-six guests on Thanksgiving Day.

When I brought up this situation to our therapist[16] many years

---

[16] We saw a therapist for a while because my wife was having a problem doing what I told her. She, for some strange reason, did not see me as the boss, the top dog, the big cheese, the big kahuna, the head honcho, leader of the pack, captain of the ship, or in charge of her in any way, even though she had taken that vow to love and <u>obey</u>. It took eight years for the therapist to explain to her how to get me to stop telling her what to do. So now that I have been set straight by my wife and the therapist, I just do what I am told.

ago, he suggested that I do the cooking while my wife write her dissertation. Brilliant! Eventually I took over the cooking completely and my wife got her PhD.

Every year for Thanksgiving, I have relished putting on a spread. I cook over ten dishes and lay them out for my family and guests to enjoy. And every year one of those guests gives me the same comment. "Why do you cook so much food?" Not "Wow, that was some Thanksgiving dinner" or "You really have outdone yourself again." Or even, "Ron you are such a fantastic cook." No. It's "Why do you cook so much food?" Thanks a lot, Mom.

I wonder if Mozart's mother said, "Amadeus, why does your Piano Concerto No. 24 in C minor have so many notes?" Did Michaelangelo's mom ask why he painted so much stuff on that ceiling? Did Dr. Martin Luther King's mom question the words he used in his 'I Have a Dream' speech? And did Jesus's mom ask why he miraculously fed 5,000 people and had so many leftovers?

Cooking is my love language. It is in many ways, my work of art. A few years ago, I did something different for Thanksgiving. It started with buying all the ingredients the night before. Scallion, thyme, onions, mushroom soup, three types of cheeses, creamed corn, cranberry sauce, turkey and ham, just to name a few. I seasoned the roast beef and turkey and placed them in the fridge to marinate.

Early the next morning I started my symphony. It began with the roast beef on the fire and the turkey in the oven. Then I mixed the ingredients needed for the corn soufflé, green bean casserole and macaroni and cheese.

It's much better this way really. At least that's what they both tell me, and I don't have the strength to fight.

Hours later there were four pots on the fire, five dishes in the oven, three platters in the fridge cooling, and one in the microwave on slow cook. I opened a bottle of Merlot, poured a small amount into one of my gravies and a large amount into a wine glass. I turned up the music and danced around the kitchen, simmering, basting, stirring, and flipping. I even do stuff to the food. No one is watching me, and I feel so happy to be in my element. I am in my world, doing my thing, preparing my masterpiece, and feeling quite at home. Maybe it's the wine you say. I say it's the recipe that works for me. A little cooking, a little music, a little smelling the aroma of my creation, and lots of anticipation for when it will be time to eat. I take out all the dishes, lay them on the counter, slice the turkey and roast beef, place the gravy in a bowl, and lay out the utensils.

And now it is time for my guests to arrive. She walks out of her room at the end of the hallway, and down to the dining room. She looks beautiful and sexy. She is the one and only guest I have invited to this dinner. Her essence is joyous and sincere, revealing a truly beautiful soul who is compelled to love with every molecule of her being. She is the one who reminds me daily why I was born, and why I need to live life with hope, joy, and passion. I have given my best effort for her and her only. I know she can be counted on to applaud my efforts and express her deep appreciation. To her, it is perfect. Every dish is a masterpiece, every mouthful succulent, every moment is cherished.

We sit and eat. No stress. No pretense. No having to act proper. I can be myself. I am with someone who knows me better than anyone in the world and thinks I am just the best. The best husband, the best performer, the best cook, the best friend, and even the best clown. With every bite she takes, she comments on the taste, articulating specific sensations and expressing her delight at having so many different dishes to choose from.

No other person can motivate me to use my talents like she does. It is in her blood to cheer people on and to encourage them in their efforts. Whatever I do in my next act I know that she will be my biggest fan and most loyal supporter. That sets me free to do my thing –whatever my thing turns out to be.

Many of us want to use our talents for good, to enrich the lives of others, to put a smile on someone's face and even to bring them laughter. Why is there so much criticism of our best efforts? Why is there so little applause and so much heckling? Why are there so few who embrace our gifts and encourage us along the way? Our individuality should be celebrated, our worldview valued, and our uniqueness embraced. When I was born nobody cared what I was thinking. I was accepted into the world, drool and all. The demands were few and the accolades, many. What happened? Somewhere along the line things got ugly, errors pointed out, mistakes criticized.

Many of us are starving for love and appreciation. We have been beaten down by life and trampled on by society. We cannot be ourselves because we fear we are just not good enough. We have to wear what people think we should wear and act like people think we should act.

We are expected to line up with the rest of the pack and walk straight, no fooling around. It's conform or be thrown out of the party. Behave or be gone. Speak a certain way, dress a certain way, and act a certain way, as if there is only one way.

I say I'm not complying. I'm a sixty-plus-year-old man who likes bunny rabbits, puppets, reading, performing magic, watching movies, making kids laugh and clowning around.

My wife is a class act and the reason I am still in the show. I can be heckled, misjudged and harassed and come home holding my head up high, my Beanie hat still firmly attached to my head, knowing I have at least one other human being who considers me to be significant. With her, I can truly be myself. And that's no joke.

Dear Dad

It was Christmas day, 1988, and my family was gathered at my home in Miami to celebrate the holiday. We were opening presents when everyone noticed Dad sitting with a big smile and what seemed to be tears on his face as he held a gift on his lap.

"Dad, aren't you going to open that?" I asked, knowing how much he would appreciate the VCR that was underneath the festive wrapping paper. We had all seen Dad savor these types of situations. He had often refused to emulate everyone else's unceremonious destruction of their carefully wrapped presents and was known to proceed with deliberate calculation. It was not unusual to see him hold an unopened letter longer than it would take most of us to write one. But on this occasion, the family members surrounding Dad could not take the suspense any longer and I complained on behalf of the group, "Come on Dad, open the gift."

"I am enjoying the moment, leave me alone." His voice was weak. Partially because he was feeble but also because he was emotionally drained by the heaviness of the moment. His fingers fiddled with the wrapping paper, tearing a few inches off, pausing, then an inch more. During the same time, the kids that were present had ripped open, played with, and discarded several of their gifts. Finally, Dad had torn the paper back enough, so the words 'Sharp VCR' appeared, and his face took a turn toward pained joy.

"This is perfect. Just what I wanted," he said, "I just wish I could really enjoy it."

Taping a favorite TV show, watching a rental movie, and playing family videos were all things my dad wanted to do. For years he had admired the technology that a video recording device offered. This was a luxury he would never have purchased for himself but would really appreciate. We all knew that when we pooled our finances to get Dad his own VCR. But watching him hold his gift it was clear something was wrong.

Two months later, in February of 1999, my father lay in a hospital bed that had been set up in the den of his Miami home, sharing his last thoughts with each of his children. The VCR sat, partially opened in its box, a reminder of how things can go from valuable to useless. Colon cancer had run amuck through his body and was about to eat away the last of his life and no electronic device could erase this reality.

He called for me and I approached his bedside to say my goodbye. On his face was an expression I had become familiar with. Yes Dad, I know, if only I would apply myself, I could really do things. I know you are supposed to remember the last words of a dying father, but I don't. I think it is because I was not prepared to let him die and somehow thought he would make a comeback. So, I let my dad go without paying close attention. But his message was so true and his example so clear that I couldn't escape forever. It wasn't what he said to me on his deathbed that finally reached down and arrested me. It was what he lived for the seventy years he was here on this earth. Now that I am almost grown up, I have come to value what my dad was trying to impart. Over the years the slouching took a toll on my life. It caused my back to hurt and my will to weaken. Slouching has been responsible for more than 50 extra pounds of fat and a flood of medical ailments. Slouching on my couch almost every night with a bag of potato chips and a soda became a visual that was systemic of my larger failures. I wasn't paying attention. I was not giving my best.

Finally, his message began to take hold and I started sitting up.

Sitting up made me feel like eating vegetables over potato chips, and fruit instead of donuts and drinking water instead of sodas. When I started sitting up, I heard a voice that said get up and go walking. When I started walking the same voice told me to dust off my tennis racket and hit a ball on the wall at the park across the street. I sat up and found that the air was fresher and the view clearer those two inches above the slouched position. For so many years I took life for granted, thinking that things would just fall into place without effort, without any sacrifice. But as I lounged, life became a burden and the pain more unbearable. Sitting up has meant I am paying attention to my purpose, my talents, and my life. It took over 50 years of living to understand the concept of applying myself completely to that which I was doing. That it did not matter so much what I did – it mattered how well I did it.

I remember as a teenager I had a drum set for a while, lent to me by one of my sister's suitors. At the time I thought this nice fella really liked me and wanted to share his drumming hobby with me. Now that he is my brother-in-law, I know I was used in order to get to my sister, and I think he was a genius. Almost every day I would spend hours drumming and I am sure to my father it just sounded like a lot of noise. It was. More than fifteen years later I was playing the drums in a church worship band. My father was present one night and came up to me after the service. "That was so beautiful," he said. "Your drum playing was heavenly. When you hit those cymbals, it was like the angels were playing for God." I remember the soft tone of his voice as he spoke and the pleasant smile on his face. He had seen me take my love for drumming to where I could now apply it to something worthwhile. It was no longer just a noise. It was a symphony to his ears.

I was thirty-one when my father died of colon cancer. Way too young to appreciate his essence and way too immature and self-absorbed to express any gratitude. So recently I wrote him a letter, and every so often I find myself reading it aloud in the hope that I will move a step closer to following in his footsteps. Even if my walk is less serious and more funny. Dad would have been so proud to see me clown around. Now that I have committed myself to first-class clowning. Now that I am sitting up.

Tear-Stained Letter

Dear Dad, I cannot believe you have been gone now for more than 30 years. When I was with you in person, I was so young and filled with confidence, knowledge, and answers and completely oblivious to how little I really knew. I remember you tried so honorably to tell me how much potential I had. You would look at me admiringly when I played soccer, spoke at church, or drove that go-cart around the track. You stood tall and straight and walked with such dignity and I was never able to match your stature. You lived life with such devotion and sacrifice and gave so much to the people you loved. Dad, I am sorry that I did not listen then. I am sorry I did not see you for what you were. I was blind to your kindness, deaf to your compassion, and oblivious to your love.

I wish that you had the chance to get to know the very special woman I married and to have enjoyed her company. You are both gifts to mankind, filled with so much goodness it oozes out and infects those who come close. She has taught me so much about listening to people and paying attention to their suffering. I would treat you so differently and focus on every word you say. I would follow my wife's example and ask you about your life, and your feelings and appreciate your insights. I would honor you more, respect you more, love you more, and criticize you less.

You would be pleased to know she has picked up where you left off and challenged me to dig deep down and put my talents to good use. When you came to stay in our home for a few months back in 1989, you would hear my wife coming home from work and say, "I hear those little feet." You acknowledged her in ways that even I as her husband did not. I didn't hear her little feet. I had the music in my head up too loud.

Dad, from this moment on, I want to commit to trying to live up to your standard of distinction and achievement in everything I do. To have your voice, your spirit, and your memory directing me toward a higher level of excellence. My selfish, immature behavior will be a thing of the past and I will be what I was created to be. I will finally heed your words and apply myself to using my talents for good. You have always been an excellent father and I am hoping it is not too late for me to be your excellent son. Thank you for all that you have taught me, for all that you did for me, for all that you mean to me. Although I did not say these things to you when you were alive, right beside me, to look at and bask in your pleasant, glowing smile, I sense that what I am doing now is somehow reverberating through the universe and stirring me toward excellence.

I have to end this letter as I just heard a door slam outside. The dog is barking at the front door and if I listen carefully and sit up and pay attention, I will "hear those little feet" walking up the driveway. My wife is coming home from a world of challenge and stress. I want her to have a man who has finally learned to be more like his dad. The best man I have ever known.

Your eternally grateful son, Ronnie

The Big Finale

I stood in front of more than one hundred 2 through 8-year-olds and started performing my regular warm-up routine when I had an epiphany of sorts. When I was the same age as some of these kids I thought, I had gone to the circus for the first time and laughed so hard I thought I would pee my pants. How many experiences have impacted us in such a dynamic way that we remember them almost 50 years later? It was entirely possible that many of these kids, because of the level and frequency of the laughter involved, would remember this day, when their kids had small kids of their own. As I considered this notion, I found myself driven to an even higher level of clowniness, shaking my body to the music, insisting that there was no dancing allowed in the show, and asking the kids who were clearly laughing at me – "Are you laughing at me?" The kids were responding with greater intensity than I had ever observed. I decided to try and take it all in. To watch the kids even as I performed. Soon, I noticed a small boy in the front row whose laugh was one of those that is so contagious, everyone within hearing distance was compelled to laugh too. I looked directly at him, put my hands on my hips, narrowed my eyes, furrowed my brows, and in a tone that was seriously funny I said – "Hey, stop laughing at me?"

He was now lying prostrate on the floor, his body shaking and his fists pounding the carpet like it was a piñata. This in turn caused me to shake my behind with such intensity I thought I would need hip surgery. The room was filled with so much laughter I felt like crying, which I knew if I succumbed to would bring an abrupt end to the laughter. But the whole scene brought me to a serious realization. I was meant to do this. I was born with a unique gift.

From the early days of man and throughout all of history people have needed comic relief from their problems, their pain, and their sorrows and I was born to bring this type of relief. What a relief. I could accept my seemingly trite vocation as a much-needed service to humanity. My life did mean something.

As I watched myself perform, I tried to imagine my dad laughing too. I remember that his laugh was a high-pitched falsetto sound that was as loud as it was distinct. It came from deep within and kept going on and on as if he couldn't stop even if he tried. His laugh seemed to say, live life to the fullest, enjoy the moments, appreciate the journey and be who you were meant to be.

Our show is a moment in space and time unique to each of us in which we can appreciate the mystery and the magic of our reality. We see things in a way that is unlike any other person on the face of the earth. Nobody can take our place. The fact that we will eventually disappear only adds to the illusion, making it that much more amazing. The important thing is that we have lived. We saw. We breathed. We participated in the 'Greatest Show on Earth' called 'Life.' It has been a real circus. Complete with acrobats, family, animals, music, laughter, food, danger, conflict, suspense, an audience, managers, performers, and clowns.

When my show opened, I was concerned that it was going to have a short run and a bad ending. But I have come to appreciate the wonder of it all, and like a child, I am in awe of the world we live in. Every single person in my life has brought something unique to the show, and I am glad I played a part. I recognize that my act contained many stages. Each period produced a somewhat different version of me. There were a few people who loved me throughout all my stages and some who couldn't quite accompany me through all my transformations. That I can leave behind my particular observations, for humans to read and have a good laugh, is a sign to me that I have entered a more settled stage and have stayed true to my calling.

As I get closer to my closing curtain, I have learned to appreciate that I'm somewhat silly, occasionally insightful, sometimes controversial, and seldom serious. I am thankful for those who have applauded me along the way and even for those whose critiques have pushed me to dig deeper. The way I see it, this has been one heck of a show, and for my big finale, I will disappear from this earth. In my opinion, that is when the magic truly begins. Because nobody knows the secret.

Ultimately, I have come to understand that comedy is utilizing one of life's most powerful weapons against disillusionment, so we can laugh as much as possible all the way to the end.

Epilogue

The sixth age shifts
Into the lean and slipper'd pantaloon,[17] With
spectacles[18] on nose and pouch on side, His
Youthful hose, well saved,[19] a world too wide
For his shrunk shank;[20] and his big manly voice,
Turning again toward childish treble, pipes
And whistles in his sound.
Last scene of all
That ends this strange eventful history,
Is second childishness and
mere oblivion.
Sans teeth[21] ands eyes, sans taste, sans everything
William's Shakespeare's As You Like It

<u>Here is my take on this</u>

The sixth age shifts
And we dress funny
Becoming a kid again
And then we disappear
Ronnie Carrington's As Nobody Likes it

Not long ago, I drove to visit my mother. I had not seen or
spoken to her for several years and had planned on keeping it that

---

[17] I do have the pantaloons but I try not to wear them.

[18] My spectacles as previously mentioned, cannot be found. None of them.

[19] wish I still had a youthful hose, but alas it didn't save.

[20] Yes, I do believe my shank has shrunk, but I am taking medication for
that.

[21] I have an appointment with my dentist next week to get that fixed.

139

way, when I had either an epiphany or indigestion. My mother, now 96, was living in an assisted living facility in Orlando Florida, and I was living in Morgantown, West Virginia.

Several months after my visit I decided to attend my mother's 96th birthday. Again, I had a revelation of sorts and decided to take a copy of my 'not quite completed book' and give her as a birthday present. Keep in mind that my book had not been proofed, which was proof I should not let anyone, especially my critical mother, read it.

I argued with myself, going back and forth between the virtues of sharing something so deeply personal with my mother, and the chances she would tell everyone she spoke to that her son was illiterate. Finally, the moment came, as I was leaving the party to return home, and I had to decide. I remember being tempted to just tell her I was almost finished with my book, and that I would send her a copy as soon as it was complete, but after my third beer, I somehow found the courage.

"Happy birthday, Mom!" I said and handed her the book. She was 'two sets of teeth.'[22]

Over the days and weeks to come I had many moments in which I regretted giving her my book. I thought of how much better I was going to make it, how silly I was to think it would make a good birthday gift and how she might not even read it.

Then, only 4 weeks later, I got the call. My mother had passed away. The circumstances surrounding her passing are sad but understandable. She was 96. But as I contemplated the events surrounding my final visit, I was struck by how comforting it was,

---

[22] My mother's phrase for ecstatic.

to think of her smiling, as I handed her the present.

Sometime later, the specific set of events surrounding her final moments were shared with me. The morning my mother was found unresponsive, she had a book on her lap. It was open and lying across her lifeless body. The book she was reading? *Sit Up and Stop Clowning Around.*

www.ingramcontent.com/pod-product-compliance
Lightning Source LLC
Chambersburg PA
CBHW071332150726
47997CB00002B/693